At Issue

Policing in America

Other Books in the At Issue Series

COVID-19 and Other Pandemics
Food Security
Genocide
Is America a Democracy or an Oligarchy?
The Media's Influence on Society
Money Laundering
Nuclear Anxiety
Open Borders
Partisanship
The Politicization of the Supreme Court

Policing in America

Kathryn Roberts, Book Editor

Published in 2022 by Greenhaven Publishing, LLC
353 3rd Avenue, Suite 255, New York, NY 10010

First Edition

Articles in Greenhaven Publishing anthologies are often edited for length to meet page requirements. In addition, original titles of these works are changed to clearly present the main thesis and to explicitly indicate the author's opinion. Every effort is made to ensure that Greenhaven Publishing accurately reflects the original intent of the authors. Every effort has been made to trace the owners of the copyrighted material.

Cover image: Michael Dechev/Shutterstock.com

Library of Congress Cataloging-in-Publication Data

Names: Roberts, Kathryn, 1990– editor.
Title: Policing in America / Kathryn Roberts, book editor.
Description: First edition. | New York : Greenhaven Publishing, 2022. | Series: At issue | Includes bibliographical references and index. | Audience: Ages 15+ | Audience: Grades 10–12 | Summary: "Curated anthology of diverse viewpoints examining all sides of policing in America through careful examination of relevant facts and opinions" — Provided by publisher.
Identifiers: LCCN 2020049128 | ISBN 9781534508095 (library binding) | ISBN 9781534508088 (paperback) | ISBN 9781534508101 (ebook)
Subjects: LCSH: Police—United States—Juvenile literature. | Law enforcement—United States—Juvenile literature. | Police brutality—United States—Juvenile literature. | Criminal justice, Administration of—United States—Juvenile literature.
Classification: LCC HV8139 .P66 2022 | DDC 363.20973—dc23
LC record available at https://lccn.loc.gov/2020049128

Manufactured in the United States of America

Website: http://greenhavenpublishing.com

Contents

Introduction

Policing in the United States has never been more relevant or more controversial than it is today. But first, consider where modern police departments originated. The beginnings of what we today consider to be policing in this country date back to colonial times. In 1636, Boston, then capital of the Massachusetts Bay Colony, established a "night watch" comprised of community volunteers whose primary duty was to warn of impending danger. The first "day watch" was established in Philadelphia in 1833, with New York following in 1844, as a supplement to its new municipal police force. By 1880, all major cities in the US had municipal police forces in place.

But it's the origination of police forces in the Southern states that explains the divisiveness that exists today between local communities and the police. In 1704, the Carolina colonies created the first "Slave Patrol," whose functions were to chase down, apprehend, and return to their owners enslaved people who had run away; provide a form of organized terror to deter revolts of enslaved people; and maintain a form of discipline over the enslaved for the violation of any plantation rules. Following the Civil War, these patrols evolved into the modern Southern police departments, primarily as a means of controlling formerly enslaved people and enforcing the Jim Crow segregation laws.

As policing evolved, many departments were modeled after inherently racist forces around the world, including the all-white occupation force placed in the Philippine Islands following the Spanish-American War of 1898, or the Texas Rangers, which were originally created as a semi-official group of vigilantes used to suppress Mexican communities and drive the Commanche—Native Americans whose historic territory consisted of most of present-day northwest Texas and eastern New Mexico—off their lands.

In Los Angeles, California, the Los Angeles Police Department (LAPD) motto is "To Protect and to Serve," a motto that is commonly associated with policing across the country. But do modern police departments "protect and serve" all people in the United States? And do modern police departments "protect and serve" all people in the United States equally?

The New York City Police Department (NYPD) implemented a practice of temporarily detaining, questioning, and searching civilians and suspects on the streets for weapons and other contraband, a policy known as "stop-and-frisk." Between 2003 and 2013, more than 100,000 stops were made each year, with over 685,000 made in 2011. The stops became subject of a racial profiling controversy, as almost 75 percent of individuals stopped through the program were people of color, even though African Americans and Latinos make up only half of New York City's population. Additionally, the bulk of the people stopped were minors and young people in their early twenties.

In 2010, New York City police officer Adrian Schoolcraft documented 2008 and 2009 orders from NYPD officials to search and arrest Black people in Brooklyn's Bedford-Stuyvesant neighborhood, and after being forced out of his position and involuntarily committed to a psychiatric hospital, he released his documentation to the *Village Voice* newspaper. Afterward, the New York Civil Liberties Union, LatinoJustice PRLDEF, and the Bronx Defenders filed a federal class action against the program, which studies showed found no evidence of its effectiveness in actually dropping crime rates.

Since the 2014 killing of Michael Brown in Ferguson, Missouri, police brutality and the killing of unarmed African Americans has been in the spotlight, along with the question of how it's possible to hold police accountable. Are body cameras the answer? More transparent access to police personnel files?

With the establishment of the Black Lives Matter movement and the subsequent response with the Blue Lives Matter movement, there have been questions posed about how to move forward in the United States in a way that does not involve the deaths of unarmed, untried people of color.

In 2020 in Minneapolis, Minnesota, George Floyd was killed for allegedly trying to use a counterfeit $20 bill, igniting protests across the United States and, indeed, around the globe in June and the following summer months, bringing the question of police brutality to the forefront of the 2020 presidential election.

And there is also the question of what police can do to better relate to the community, including providing incentives for police officers to actually live in the cities they serve—which by and large, police officers cannot afford to do.

At Issue: Policing in America examines a relevant and contentious issue that threatens to divide much of the country today. The authors of the diverse viewpoints that follow take into consideration not just the connections between race and police brutality in the United States, but what solutions can be created and implemented on both a national level and a local one, to minimize violence, create more transparency, and create communities that serve all people, no matter the skin color.

1

How to Fix American Policing

Ken Armstrong

Ken Armstrong is a former staff writer and a Pulitzer Prize–winning investigative reporter who previously worked at the Seattle Times *and* Chicago Tribune, *where his work helped prompt the Illinois governor to suspend executions and later empty death row. He has been the McGraw Professor of Writing at Princeton and a Nieman Fellow at Harvard.*

In the following viewpoint, Ken Armstrong of the Marshall Project, a nonpartisan, nonprofit organization created to sustain a sense of national urgency about the US criminal justice system, poses questions about the potential reforms available to improve the relationship between the police and the Black communities they serve. Through efforts involving a national standard for use of force, greater transparency within both police departments and the justice system, the importance of human contact, not seeking out confrontation, the formation of special prosecutors, and making efforts to diversify police forces, Armstrong explores not just potential reforms but also reforms that have seen positive change throughout police departments across the United States.

"How to Fix American Policing," by Ken Armstrong, The Marshall Project, July 13, 2016. Reprinted by permission.

The question isn't new, but after last week it seems more urgent than ever: What reforms are available to improve the relationship between police and the black communities they serve?

That question has figured in policy platforms issued by a variety of groups, from leaders of the Black Lives Matter movement (that platform is called Campaign Zero), to the President's Task Force on 21st Century Policing to the NAACP. Some platforms apply to a single jurisdiction, such as the proposals for the New York City Police Department issued by Communities United for Police Reform. Some ideas come from academics. Some come from community advocates or the ranks of law enforcement. Some ideas have been pitched for decades while others have surfaced in recent years. Many have been discussed at national conferences on this question, hosted by the Department of Justice.

Last week, the tension between black and blue, as some have phrased it, sparked protests and vigils around the country, following the shooting deaths of Alton Sterling in Baton Rouge, La.; Philando Castile in Falcon Heights, Minn.; and police officers Patrick Zamarripa, Michael Smith, Michael Krol, Lorne Ahrens and Brent Thompson in Dallas.

What follows is a canvass of proposed reforms, including ones renewed in the aftermath of last week's killings:

A National Standard for Use of Force

The United States has about 18,000 police departments, including local, state and federal agencies. What it does not have is a national standard for when the police in all those departments can or should use force. Guidelines vary for the use of guns, Tasers, choke-holds and other kinds of force, as does emphasis on restraint or de-escalation.

Instead of following a uniform policy—something that could be enforced by a threat to withhold federal funding—departments adopt their own, sometimes updating them only in the wake of controversy. The Baltimore Police Department revised its policy two weeks ago, following the death in 2015 of Freddie Gray, who suffered fatal spinal injuries as he was being transported in a police van. US Customs and Border Protection revised its policy in 2014, following an investigation by the *Arizona Republic* into dozens of deaths at the hands of Border Patrol agents and CBP officers.

The NAACP has supported this proposal for years, and renewed its call after last week's shootings. Hillary Clinton also voiced support last week for national guidelines. As a reflection of how long this has been discussed, Rep. John Conyers of Michigan introduced legislation in 2000 that included national standards for use of force, but the bill died in committee.

State laws on the use of force vary in the circumstances under which police can be prosecuted for using lethal force improperly. The *Seattle Times* published an investigation last year of Washington's statute—"the nation's most restrictive law on holding officers accountable." The law, passed in 1986, allows prosecution only if an officer acted with "evil intent." The *Seattle Times* found that in 213 fatal police encounters from 2005 to 2014, only one officer was charged—and he was acquitted. A bill to change the state's law was subsequently introduced, but drew opposition from law enforcement and failed to make it out of committee.

More Data, Greater Transparency

As our Tom Meagher reported two months ago ("13 Important Questions About Criminal Justice We Can't Answer"), the criminal justice system, including policing, suffers from a stunning data gap. How many shootings are there in America? We can't say for sure. How many police officers are investigated for misconduct? We don't know. How often do police stop pedestrians or drivers? Ditto.

When Congress has tried to address elements of this—requiring states to report on people killed in police custody, for example—its efforts have often been defined by a lack of follow-through. What data the government does collect is often riddled with holes. The media, meanwhile, has attempted to fill in the gaps, with investigations on police shootings by the *Washington Post*, the *Guardian* and ProPublica.

Proposals to improve police-community relations often emphasize the need not only for accurate information, but to ensure that the information is shared freely with the public. But transparency has been as elusive as sound data. In the last few days—with national attention focused largely on the shootings in Dallas, Minnesota and Louisiana—developments elsewhere have reflected the resistance towards access in some law enforcement and government circles. Last year, the White House invited police departments to commit to sharing more of their statistics with the public. As of April, only 53 jurisdictions had signed up.

The governor of North Carolina signed a bill restricting public access to video from police body and dashboard cameras. "Shameful," a representative of the ACLU of North Carolina called the law. In Illinois, an appeals court ruled in favor of releasing decades' worth of complaints against Chicago police; in that case the Fraternal Order of Police had previously secured an injunction, blocking the release. And in California, a local judge ruled that the City of Hayward had charged too much for access to police camera footage from a Black Lives Matter protest in which officers could be heard saying such things as, "They are fucking animals." The city had billed $3,247 for the video. The judge knocked the charge down to $1.While the push for police body cameras has picked up momentum—a little more than half of the country's major cities have committed to them—there have also been other measures designed to document police interactions and make them more transparent, such as the proposal to require New York City police officers to provide citizens with their name and rank, even if not asked.

Human Contact

Last week the *Oregonian* published a story about a black actor and a white police captain in Portland that captured the good that can come from something so simple as two people meeting to share their experiences. The actor talked of being stopped by police time and again; one time, in a traffic stop over a broken taillight, four police cars pulled up, making him fear for his life. The captain talked of making such stops, of approaching a car in the dark and the fear of someone reaching for an officer's gun. Both men left with a greater understanding—a principal goal of policing reforms that are centered on building trust by bringing the police and the community together.

The idea of community policing is to get police out of their squad cars, out of their station houses, and into the community where they're able to walk, talk and listen. The police department in Redlands, California, has embraced this model for years. Scott Thomson, the police chief of Camden County, N.J., says, "We established a culture from very, very early on that the relationship that would bind us with our people was one based upon building the community first and enforcing the law second." Police interactions with the public shouldn't be confined to "moments of crisis," says Thomson, who wants officers to be more guardian than warrior.

Coffee with a Cop, a program that does just what the title says, started five years ago in Hawthorne, Calif., and has since spread to all 50 states. In some places, such as Boston, police have taken to driving ice cream trucks and handing out cold treats to kids. Some departments encourage officers to not only work in the community, but to live in it. Detroit, Baltimore, Atlanta, West Valley City, Utah, Chattanooga, Tenn., and other cities have taken to offering financial incentives, be it cheap home prices, discounted rents, cash bonuses or tax credits, to officers who choose to live in the place they police.

Don't Seek Out Confrontation

Many police shootings have started with stops over the smallest of infractions. So one category of proposed reforms calls for a drawdown in the policing of comparatively petty matters. Last week a writer for the *Atlantic* offered one proposal along these lines: Instead of having police pull over cars for a broken taillight—and then approach the driver's window, initiating the kind of exchange that can go so terribly wrong, as it did with Philando Castile in Minnesota and Walter Scott in South Carolina—how about the police photograph the license plate, then dash off a ticket to the registered owner?

Alton Sterling was hawking CDs in Baton Rouge, Eric Garner was selling loose cigarettes on Staten Island. Both died at the hands of police. Aggressive enforcement against street vendors in effect criminalizes poverty, the head of a non-profit that works with vendors told the *Washington Post*. A Salon headline called it "criminalizing the hustle."

The list of proposed solutions from Campaign Zero includes an end to broken windows policing, in which minor crimes are targeted, and an end to for-profit policing, marked by arrest or ticket quotas and excessive fines. *Mother Jones* coined a term—"policiteering"—for enforcement that seems directed more at revenue generation than public safety, citing Samuel DuBose in Cincinnati and Sandra Bland in Texas as examples of minor traffic stops that escalated. In some states speed traps proliferate.

While some reform advocates call for an end to such approaches as broken-windows and stop-and-frisk policing, middle ground can be found, in which police use the tactics less zealously. "Violations of public order rules almost always call for education, reminders, and warnings rather than arrests," a University of Michigan professor wrote in a broken-windows commentary for the Marshall Project. And New York Police Commissioner William Bratton told our Simone Weichselbaum last year that stop-and-frisk is "an essential tool of American policing," but has been used too extensively, "like a doctor treating a patient with cancer with chemotherapy." The NYPD's use of stop-and-frisk has declined from a peak of nearly 700,000 in 2011 to about 25,000 last year. "It's a tool that needs to be used with great precision," Bratton said.

In Chicago, meanwhile, Injustice Watch reported last week on how that city's use of stop-and-frisk has often alienated communities of color. In just four months in 2014, the Chicago

Police Department made about 250,000 stops that did not lead to arrest—and 72 percent of the people stopped were black.

From Special Prosecutors to Diversified Police Forces

Around the country a host of other reform proposals have been raised, including:

- Use a special prosecutor to handle cases of alleged police misconduct: When police and prosecutors work together in the same jurisdiction, questions inevitably surface about whether prosecutors can be impartial in handling these cases. A special prosecutor creates distance and, at a minimum, helps with public perception.
- Make police departments more diverse, which, for many police departments, has been a struggle.
- Train police on implicit racial bias and de-escalation: As reported by NPR and others after last week's shootings, one of the nation's leaders in de-escalation training has been the Dallas Police Department, which has seen a dramatic decrease in such metrics as complaints alleging excessive force.
- Demilitarize the police: Already a point of contention, the issue of police dressed in battle gear and wielding military armament received renewed attention last week, due in large part to one particular photo taken in Baton Rouge.

2

Prison Rape Allegations Are on the Rise

Alysia Santo

Alysia Santo is a staff writer for the Marshall Project. Her investigative reporting on the criminal justice system has appeared in the New York Times, *the* Los Angeles Times, USA Today, *and elsewhere. She was a finalist for the Livingston Award in both 2016 and 2017 and a runner-up for the John Jay College/H.F. Guggenheim Prize for Excellence in Criminal Justice Reporting in 2017 and 2019.*

In the following viewpoint, Alysia Santo investigates the reasoning behind the rise of rape allegations in prisons in the United States. In 2012, the US Justice Department issued its first set of national standards for how detention centers must give inmates ways to report sexual abuse and for staff to be made available to investigate the allegations. According to the Bureau of Justice Statistics, from 2011 to 2015, the number of allegations of sexual assault increased more than 180 percent since these standards were implemented, though the report also shows that corrections administrators rarely decide that the allegations in question actually occurred.

"Prison Rape Allegations Are on the Rise," by Alysia Santo, The Marshall Project. July 25, 2018. Reprinted by permission.

For a long time in the popular imagination, prison rape was, quite literally, a joke. Most cop shows could be counted on for a biting aside or two about dropping soap in a jail shower. But in Washington, some prisoner advocates took the problem seriously, pushing for the passage of the federal Prison Rape Elimination Act in 2003. Almost a decade later, in 2012, the Justice Department issued its first set of national standards requiring that detention facilities not only give inmates multiple ways to report sexual abuse but also investigate every allegation.

Prison rape is far from being eliminated, and there have been complaints for years that the law lacks real teeth. But new numbers released Wednesday show there has been at least one big change since 2012: sexual assault behind bars is being reported more—a lot more.

"I see this is a clear sign that prisoners are starting to trust the system, rather than an indication that sexual abuse in detention is skyrocketing," said Lovissa Stannow, the executive director of Just Detention International, the leading advocacy organization trying to curb prison rape.

In 2011, before the national standards were issued, there were 8,768 allegations of sexual assault and harassment nationwide. By the end of 2015, that total had jumped to 24,661, a leap of more than 180 percent, according to the federal Bureau of Justice Statistics, which compiles the numbers it collects from corrections departments.

Still, the report shows, corrections administrators rarely decide that the alleged attacks actually happened. The number of accusations found to be true increased only slightly, while the number of allegations that were eventually found to be false or inconclusive skyrocketed.

Of the 61,316 completed investigations from 2012 through 2015, corrections officials decided that 5,187 allegations—or about 8.5 percent—were found to be true.

For the remaining vast majority of allegations, corrections officials determined that either the report was false or there was not enough evidence to decide either way.

Stannow was skeptical that inmates are making such high numbers of fake accusations. "Prisoners have nothing to gain from filing false sex abuse reports," she said. Corrections officials often start with the assumption that a report is false, particularly when it's against a colleague, Stannow said. "There's a very strong tendency to close ranks," she said.

The new data show that allegations made by inmates against staffers made up the majority of reports in 2015—58 percent—while constituting less than half of all the allegations later proven to be true—42 percent.

The report covers local and Indian country jails; federal, state and private prisons; military lockup; and Immigration and Customs Enforcement detention facilities.

Since 2003, the Prison Rape Elimination Act has required the government to collect statistics two ways: prison administrators submit their official findings, which was the basis of the report released Wednesday, and inmates complete anonymous surveys. The last prisoner survey was conducted in 2012. The BJS has estimated that more than 200,000 inmates are sexually abused in American detention facilities annually.

"We know there are many victims who don't feel comfortable coming forward, and correction administrators only know what comes to their attention," said Allen Beck, BJS senior statistical advisor. "Right now, what we're seeing can be largely accounted for by improved record-keeping and enhanced sensitivity on the part of inmates and corrections officials on issues of sexual victimization."

Beck said better investigative techniques may have also contributed to the rise in the number of accusations found to be false. Those cases may have been found to be inconclusive in the past, he said.

The report lacked details it has had in the past, such as the gender of the alleged victims and perpetrators, the sanctions imposed, and the most common locations where sexual abuse allegedly took place.

"It's really difficult to draw any conclusions from this," said Pat Nolan, a former California politician who was imprisoned in the 1990s and became a member of the National Prison Rape Elimination Commission, which helped promulgate the standards. "One of the ideas of these surveys is to give us information to try to prevent future assaults, and that's totally missing from this."

Those details are expected to be released next year, BJS said.

3

Body-Worn Cameras: What the Evidence Tells Us

Brett Chapman

Brett Chapman is a social science analyst in the Office of Research, Evaluation, and Technology at the United States National Institute of Justice.

In the following viewpoint, Brett Chapman details the evolution of modern policing, starting with the development of Sir Robert Peel's Nine Principles of Law Enforcement in 1829. Among others, the second principle emphasizes police activities and duties dependent upon public approval and the ability to maintain public respect. Almost 200 years later, the police's ability to fight crime effectively continues to depend on the public's perception of the legitimacy of the actions of officers. With the subsequent use of force within the US that has gained traction within national media, there has been an emphasis on the importance of using body-worn cameras to enable law enforcement officers to operate with more transparency. Chapman additionally explores current research findings regarding the use and effectiveness of these cameras.

"Body-Worn Cameras: What the Evidence Tells Us," by Brett Chapman, National Institute of Justice, November 14, 2018.

In 1829, Sir Robert Peel—regarded by many as the father of modern policing—developed what came to be known as the Nine Principles of Law Enforcement, which were given to British law enforcement officers as general instructions. Peel's second principle stated, "The ability of the police to perform their duties is dependent upon *public approval* of police existence, actions, behavior and the ability of the police to secure and maintain *public respect*."[1]

Nearly 200 years later, Peel's principle still holds true: The ability of law enforcement to fight crime effectively continues to depend on the public's perception of the legitimacy of the actions of officers. A number of recent civil disturbances across the United States subsequent to instances of lethal use of force by officers highlight the ongoing challenges in maintaining the public's perceptions of law enforcement legitimacy, particularly as it concerns the use of force.

Body-worn cameras have been viewed as one way to address these challenges and improve law enforcement practice more generally. The technology, which can be mounted on an officer's eyeglasses or chest area, offers real-time information when used by officers on patrol or other assignments that bring them into contact with members of the community. Another benefit of body-worn cameras is their ability to provide law enforcement with a surveillance tool to promote officer safety and efficiency and prevent crime.

This technology has diffused rapidly across the United States. In 2013, approximately one-third of US municipal police departments had implemented the use of body-worn cameras.[2] Members of the general public also continue to embrace the technology. But what does the research tell us? Current studies suggest that body-worn cameras may offer benefits for law enforcement, but additional research is needed to more fully understand the value of the technology for the field.

Potential Benefits

Proponents of body-worn cameras point to several potential benefits.

Better Transparency

First, body-worn cameras may result in better transparency and accountability and thus may improve law enforcement legitimacy. In many communities, there is a lack of trust and confidence in law enforcement. This lack of confidence is exacerbated by questions about encounters between officers and community members that often involve the use of deadly or less-lethal force. Video footage captured during these officer-community interactions might provide better documentation to help confirm the nature of events and support accounts articulated by officers and community residents.[3]

Increased Civility

Body-worn cameras may also result in higher rates of citizen compliance to officer commands during encounters and fewer complaints lodged against law enforcement. Citizens often change their behavior toward officers when they are informed that the encounter is being recorded. This "civilizing effect" may prevent certain situations from escalating to levels requiring the use of force and also improve interactions between officers and citizens.[4]

Quicker Resolution

Body-worn cameras may lead to a faster resolution of citizen complaints and lawsuits that allege excessive use of force and other forms of officer misconduct. Investigations of cases that involve inconsistent accounts of the encounter from officers and citizens are often found to be "not sustained" and are subsequently closed when there is no video footage nor independent or corroborating witnesses. This, in turn, can decrease the public's trust and confidence in law enforcement and increase perceptions that claims of abuse brought against officers will not be properly addressed.

Video captured by body-worn cameras may help corroborate the facts of the encounter and result in a quicker resolution.

Corroborating Evidence

Footage captured may also be used as evidence in arrests or prosecutions. Proponents have suggested that video captured by body-worn cameras may help document the occurrence and nature of various types of crime, reduce the overall amount of time required for officers to complete paperwork for case files, corroborate evidence presented by prosecutors, and lead to higher numbers of guilty pleas in court proceedings.

Training Opportunities

The use of body-worn cameras also offers potential opportunities to advance policing through training. Law enforcement trainers and executives can assess officer activities and behavior captured by body-worn cameras—either through self-initiated investigations or those that result from calls for service—to advance professionalism among officers and new recruits. Finally, video footage can provide law enforcement executives with opportunities to implement new strategies and assess the extent to which officers carry out their duties in a manner that is consistent with the assigned initiatives.

Current Research Findings

The increasing use of body-worn cameras by law enforcement agencies has significantly outpaced the body of research examining the relationship between the technology and law enforcement outcomes. As detailed below, although early evaluations of this technology had limitations, some notable recent research has helped advance our knowledge of the impact of body-worn cameras.

In a 2014 study funded by the Office of Justice Programs Diagnostic Center, researcher Michael White noted that earlier evaluations of body-worn cameras found a number of beneficial outcomes for law enforcement agencies.[5] The earliest studies conducted in the United Kingdom indicated that body-worn cameras resulted in positive interactions between officers and citizens and made people feel safer. Reductions in citizen complaints were noted, as were similar reductions in crime. The studies found that the use of body-worn cameras led to increases in arrests, prosecutions, and guilty pleas.[6] From an efficiency standpoint, the use of the technology reportedly enabled officers to resolve criminal cases faster and spend less time preparing paperwork, and it resulted in fewer people choosing to go to trial.

Studies that followed in the United States also provided support for body-worn cameras; however, a number of them were plagued with dubious approaches that called the findings into question. According to White, the few studies that were conducted between 2007 and 2013 had methodological limitations or were conducted in a manner that raised concerns about research independence. For example, several studies included small sample sizes or lacked proper control groups to compare officers wearing body-worn cameras with officers not wearing them. Some studies were conducted by the participating law enforcement agency and lacked an independent evaluator. Finally, a number of the studies focused narrowly on officer or citizen perceptions of body-worn cameras instead of other critical outcomes, such as citizen compliance and officer or citizen behavior in instances involving use of force.

Over time, scientific rigor improved, and studies conducted in US law enforcement agencies produced findings that indicated promising support for body-worn cameras. For example, in 2014, researchers at Arizona State University (funded through the Bureau of Justice Assistance's Smart Policing Initiative) found that officers with body-worn cameras were more productive in terms of making arrests, had fewer complaints lodged against them relative to officers without body-worn cameras, and had higher numbers of citizen complaints resolved in their favor.[7] Another study conducted with the Rialto (California) Police Department noted similar decreases in citizen complaints lodged against officers wearing body-worn cameras as well as decreases in use-of-force incidents by the police.[8] In addition, Justin Ready and Jacob Young from Arizona State University found that officers with body-worn cameras were more cautious in their actions and sensitive to possible scrutiny of video footage by their superiors. Also, contrary to initial concerns, officers who wore cameras were found to have higher numbers of self-initiated contacts with community residents than officers who did not wear cameras.[9]

Recent randomized controlled trials, which are considered the scientific gold standard for evaluating programs, have also been conducted on body-worn cameras. Of the various scientific methods available, these trials have the greatest likelihood of producing sound evidence because random assignment is able to isolate a specific treatment of interest from all of the other factors that influence any given outcome. In a 2016 global, multisite randomized controlled trial, Barak Ariel and colleagues found that use-of-force incidents may be related to the discretion given to officers regarding when body-worn cameras are activated during officer-citizen encounters. The researchers found decreases in use-of-force incidents when officers activated their cameras upon arrival at the scene. Alternatively, use-of-force incidents by officers with body-worn cameras increased when the officers had the discretion to determine when to activate their cameras during citizen interactions.[10]

In 2017, with NIJ support, researchers from CNA conducted a randomized controlled trial on 400 police officers in the Las Vegas Metropolitan Police Department. The research team found that officers with body-worn cameras generated fewer use-of-force reports and complaints from citizens compared to officers without body-worn cameras. Additionally, officers with body-worn cameras issued higher numbers of arrests and citations compared to officers without body-worn cameras.[11]

More Research Is Needed

An increasing number of studies have emerged to help fill knowledge gaps in the current body of research on body-worn cameras. Researchers at George Mason University noted that 14 studies have been completed and at least 30 others are currently examining the impact of body-worn cameras on various outcomes.[12] The most common outcomes examined include the impact of body-worn cameras on the quality of officer-citizen interactions measured by the nature of the communication, displays of procedural justice and professionalism, and misconduct or corruption; use of force by officers; attitudes about body-worn cameras; citizen satisfaction with law enforcement encounters; perceptions of law enforcement and legitimacy; suspect compliance with officer commands; and criminal investigations and law enforcement-initiated activity.[13]

However, knowledge gaps still exist. The George Mason University researchers highlighted the need to examine organizational concerns regarding body-worn cameras. For example, little attention has been focused on improvements in training and organizational policies. Additional information is also needed on how body-worn cameras can help facilitate investigations of officer-involved shootings or other critical incidents, and on the value of video footage captured by body-worn cameras in court proceedings.

Current research varies by level of rigor and methods used, but the results continue to help law enforcement executives decide whether to adopt this technology in their agencies. Overall, the research on body-worn cameras suggests that the technology may offer potential benefits for law enforcement. However, the true extent of its value will depend on the continuation of research studies to keep pace with the growing adoption and implementation of body-worn cameras by law enforcement agencies in the United States.

Notes

1. Italics in quote are from original publication, *Sir Robert Peel's Principles of Law Enforcement 1829*, Durham Constabulary, Durham, England.
2. Brian A. Reaves, *Local Police Departments, 2013: Equipment and Technology*, Bulletin, Washington, DC: US Department of Justice, Bureau of Justice Statistics, July 2015, NCJ 248767, https://www.bjs.gov/content/pub/pdf/ lpd13et.pdf.

3. Michael D. White, *Police Officer Body-Worn Cameras: Assessing the Evidence*, Washington, DC: US Department of Justice, Office of Community Oriented Policing Services, 2014.
4. Changes in the behavior of citizens may result from the presence of body-worn cameras on officers coupled with citizens being informed in certain encounters that they are being recorded. However, researchers have noted that this civilizing effect is complex and additional research is needed to examine the issue.
5. White, *Police Officer Body-Worn Cameras.*
6. The use of body-worn cameras was found to be particularly helpful in improving the overall strength of prosecution cases involving domestic violence because the cameras documented the victims' demeanor and language and recorded the crime scenes and overall emotional effects on the victims.
7. Charles Katz, David Choate, Justin Ready, and Lidia Nuno, "Evaluating the Impact of Officer Worn Body Cameras in the Phoenix Police Department" (Phoenix, AZ: Center for Violence & Community Safety, Arizona State University, 2015).
8. Barak Ariel, William A. Farrar, and Alex Sutherland, "The Effect of Police Body-Worn Cameras on Use of Force and Citizens' Complaints against the Police: A Randomized Controlled Trial," *Journal of Quantitative Criminology* 31 no. 3 (2015): 509-535.
9. Justin T. Ready and Jacob T. N. Young, "The Impact of On-Officer Video Cameras on Police-Citizen Contacts: Findings from a Controlled Experiment in Mesa, AZ," *Journal of Experimental Criminology* 11 no. 3 (2015): 445-458.
10. Barak Ariel, Alex Sutherland, Darren Henstock, Josh Young, Paul Drover, Jayne Sykes, Simon Megicks, and Ryan Henderson, "Report: Increases in Police Use of Force in the Presence of Body-Worn Cameras Are Driven by Officer Discretion: A Protocol-Based Subgroup Analysis of Ten Randomized Experiments," *Journal of Experimental Criminology* 12 no. 3 (2016): 453-463.
11. Anthony Braga, James R. Coldren, William Sousa, Denise Rodriguez, and Omer Alper, *The Benefits of Body-Worn Cameras: New Findings from a Randomized Controlled Trial at the Las Vegas Metropolitan Police Department*, Washington, DC: US Department of Justice, National Institute of Justice, December 2017.
12. Cynthia Lum, Christopher Koper, Linda Merola, Amber Scherer, and Amanda Reioux, "Existing and Ongoing Body Worn Camera Research: Knowledge Gaps and Opportunities" (New York: The Laura and John Arnold Foundation, 2015).
13. Lum also noted an increase in randomized controlled trials among the growing number of body-worn camera studies.

4

Guns Make Policing in America Dangerous for Officers and Civilians Alike

Laurel Rosenhall

Laurel Rosenhall covers California politics for CalMatters, with a focus on power and personalities in the statehouse. Her stories explain political dynamics and examine how money, advocacy, and relationships shape the decisions that affect Californians. She also hosts the Force of Law podcast, which follows California's attempt to reduce police shootings. Rosenhall joined CalMatters in 2015 after more than a dozen years as a reporter for the Sacramento Bee, *where she covered state politics and education.*

The following viewpoint provides a summary of season one, episode four of the Force of Law podcast, titled "The Line." Laurel Rosenhall details how research from legal scholar Franklin Zimring shows that the rate of fatal assaults on American police officers is 25 times greater than the rate of fatal assaults on British police officers and 40 times greater than on German police officers. Additional findings show that the rate of police shootings in outside nations is a fraction of what it is within the United States. The research goes on to show that gunshots cause 97 percent of deaths of American police officers.

"Podcast: Guns Make Policing in America Dangerous—to Officers and Civilians Alike," by Laurel Rosenhall, CalMatters, July 23, 2019. This article is reprinted with permission from CalMatters, a nonprofit news organization that covers California state politics and policy.

America's embrace of civilian gun ownership makes police work more dangerous in the United States than in other developed countries, a phenomenon that in turn contributes to officers killing nearly 1,000 people each year.

That's the conclusion Franklin Zimring, a legal scholar and criminal justice expert at the University of California, Berkeley, came to after conducting a major study of killings both of police and by police. The rate of fatal assaults on American officers is 25 times greater than on British police and 40 times greater than on German police, he found. Similarly, the rate of police shootings in those nations is a tiny fraction of what it is in the US.

Zimring studied attacks on American officers over six years and found that gunshots caused more than 97 percent of their deaths.

"If I am a police officer on patrol, the threats to my life that exist are almost completely, in terms of assaults, firearms," Zimring said on Force of Law, a podcast about California's attempt to reduce police shootings.

"We have them in 100 million households. We have them in millions of cars. They make police patrolling much more dangerous in this country than in other countries. And because they are dangerous for police, police are much more dangerous and much more apt to use life-threatening force against civilians."

Officers know that any time they show up at a call, even the ones that seem most routine, they may face someone with a firearm. That's what happened to Sacramento Police Officer Tara O'Sullivan, who was gunned down last month when she arrived at a house where a domestic violence victim had asked for help. And to Davis Police Officer Natalie Corona, who was ambushed by a gunman while helping at the scene of a car accident.

These occupational hazards have loomed over the Capitol as California lawmakers have debated a bill to limit when officers can shoot—legislation responding to the death of Stephon Clark, whom police shot after mistaking the cell phone he was holding for a gun. He was not armed, but most of the people police kill are holding a gun or a knife.

Law enforcement first argued against the bill, saying it would put officers' lives at even greater risk. If they felt they had to hesitate before firing their weapons, police argued, more cops would die. After Assembly Bill 392 was amended, though, major statewide law enforcement groups stopped making that argument and dropped their opposition to the bill.

The version the Legislature passed earlier this month says police can use deadly force when "necessary in defense of human life"—and doesn't specifically define what "necessary" means. It also says that in judging whether deadly force was necessary, authorities must use the perspective of a "reasonable officer," echoing concepts in a landmark United States Supreme Court case that police view as a critical legal protection.

"That's why I was able to support it," said Assemblyman Tom Lackey, who voted against the original version of AB 392 in committee, but voted for the revised version on the Assembly floor. He's now convinced that it won't put officers in greater danger.

Lackey, a Republican from Palmdale, was a highway patrol officer for many years before being elected to the Legislature. On the Force of Law podcast, he describes losing several colleagues during his law enforcement career—in attacks, crashes and suicide.

Though policing remains a dangerous profession, the rate of on-duty deaths has dropped dramatically since 1970, according to research by Michael White, a professor at Arizona State University's school of criminology.

"Policing is a much safer profession now than it was 50 years ago," he said, due to improvements in body armor, training and trauma care.

5

The Policing of Black Americans Is Racial Harassment Funded by the State

Paul Butler

Paul Butler provides legal commentary for MSNBC and NPR and has been featured on 60 Minutes *and profiled in the* Washington Post. *A law professor at Georgetown University, he is the author of* Let's Get Free: A Hip-Hop Theory of Justice, *winner of the Harry Chapin Media Award, and* Chokehold: Policing Black Men *(both from the New Press). He has published numerous op-eds and book reviews, including in the* New York Times, *the* Washington Post, *the* Boston Globe, *and the* Los Angeles Times.

The following viewpoint showcases what author Paul Butler alleges is the "burden of proof" Black people are forced to provide while simply living their lives. Highlighting highly publicized incidents like the two African American men who had the police called on them for simply sitting at a Philadelphia-area Starbucks, Butler shows how Black people in the United States must justify their actions to the white people who make the choice to call the authorities on them. The author highlights how this is an everyday situation for people of color, especially Black people, and also that the fact that it happens with such regularity is unacceptable, even as it is a well-known facet of the current policing system.

"The Policing of Black Americans Is Racial Harassment Funded by the State," by Paul Butler, Guardian News & Media Limited, June 6, 2018. Reprinted by permission.

The Policing of Black Americans Is Racial Harassment Funded by the State

The rap group Public Enemy famously stated that "911 is a joke." But that was in 1990. These days 911 is dead serious. Anyone in the United States can dial those three numbers and summon people with guns and handcuffs to participate in their anti-black paranoia. It's racial harassment, sponsored by the government and supported by tax dollars.

When one calls 911 in New York City, the first question the dispatcher asks is "What is your emergency?" I wonder how the white people recently in the news for calling the police on black folks would have answered that question. "Two men sitting at Starbucks." "Four women golfing slowly." "Graduate student napping." "Man moving into apartment." "Women moving luggage out of a house."

The people who call the police are not the main problem. Of course those people are, to use an old-fashioned word, prejudiced. It is difficult to imagine them being made anxious by white people going about the business of their everyday lives. But this kind of racism for black people is, in fact, everyday.

This does not mean that it is acceptable: everyday racism is aggravating, health draining, and, for its survivors, labor intensive. Everyday racism requires a performance when a black person navigates white spaces. You conspicuously display your work ID. You look down on the elevator. You whistle Vivaldi.

The people who call the police can fill a black person with a productive rage or a corrosive kind of hate. In my ideal world, when people call the police on black people for no good reason, they would be taken to a public place and beaten with sticks. By black people. They are spirit murderers. But still they are not the main problem.

The main problem is the response of the state. "We'll send a squad over right away." The caller has offered a short pitch for a white supremacist fantasia, and now the dispatcher green-lights it. She sends a crew over to the set identified by the caller and the spectacle is produced.

Black people are forced, by armed officers of the government, to justify their presence. They have the burden of proof; the person who called the police is assumed to be correct. That the black person gets to make her case at all is an incremental evolution in justice from the antebellum south, where white people could and did make all manner of false accusations against blacks but black people were not allowed to be witnesses against whites in any official proceeding.

In recent cases, black people have offered excuses like "golfing," "napping" and "moving." For two African American men at the Starbucks in Philadelphia, "waiting for a friend" is deemed insufficient. The men are placed in handcuffs and taken to jail. The Philadelphia police chief, Richard Ross, says "the police did absolutely nothing wrong." Later, when the arrests created a national firestorm, the chief apologizes. He says that, as a black man, he should have known better.

What I want to say is that usually the police know better, and it does not matter. Darren Martin had the police called on him when he was just moving into a new apartment in Manhattan. A neighbor claimed he was breaking down the door and had a weapon. Martin had the presence of mind, and courage, to livestream the police response.

The six NYPD officers who reported to the scene discovered a young black man moving stuff to a fifth-floor walk-up. Still the cops put Martin through the procedure, interrogating him and forcing him to show ID. When Martin protested, the officers stood there with a stupid look on their faces. It's the "we are just doing our jobs" expression.

The sad thing is that they are exactly right. Enforcing a racialized law and order is an important function of police work in the 21st century. In my book *Chokehold*, I suggest that the problem is not bad apple cops. The problem is the system is working the way it is supposed to. The US criminal legal process is all about keeping people—especially African American men—in their place.

Even when trespassing white space is not an arrestable offense, it can occasion a fraught encounter.

The Harvard scholar Henry Louis Gates Jr wrote: "Black men swap their experiences of police encounters like war stories, and there are few who don't have more than one story to tell." The crazy thing is that Gates wrote this in 1995, long before he was arrested by the Cambridge police after a neighbor called the police to report he was trespassing on his own front porch. I have more stories than I can count. The time the police followed me when I was walking in my neighborhood and told me to go in my house to prove that I lived there. The evening I worked late and the night security guard barged into my office and demanded my work ID. Afterwards the primary emotions are anger—no matter what you do you still get judged by the color of your skin—and relief—at least you got out of this one without being arrested, beat up, or killed.

The structure that allows this cannot stand. I make that claim hopefully, as when Martin Luther King Jr said: "the arc of the moral universe curves toward justice." I also make that claim descriptively, as when King said "no lie can live forever." In *Chokehold*, I suggest ways of improving relations between the police and communities of color, including having more women and college-educated cops, who the data suggests, respond to these kind of situations more effectively. Ultimately the whole culture of policing must be transformed, from the "warrior" mentality that Barack Obama described, to one of "guardians."

It turns out that, back in 1990, when Public Enemy described 911 as a joke, they weren't even talking about the police. Their complaint was that paramedics didn't show up when they were summoned to the hood. Those were the first responders who the community would have welcomed. Long before the viral videos of police abuse, many black folks had already given up on the cops.

6

New Study Says White Police Officers Are Not More Likely to Shoot Minority Suspects

Martin Kaste

Martin Kaste is a correspondent on NPR's National Desk. He covers law enforcement and privacy. He has been focused on police and use of force since before the 2014 protests in Ferguson, Missouri, and that coverage led to the creation of NPR's Criminal Justice Collaborative. In addition to criminal justice reporting, Kaste has contributed to NPR News coverage of major world events, including the 2010 earthquake in Haiti and the 2011 uprising in Libya.

The following viewpoint is a transcript from a podcast hosted by NPR's Ari Shapiro in which NPR correspondent Martin Kaste discusses a report published in the peer-reviewed journal the Proceedings of the National Academy of Sciences *about whether or not white cops are more likely to shoot minority suspects. The study claims that they do not, but Kaste notes that there is the possibility that the study was not asking questions that truly get to the root of the continued, highly publicized instances of just that situation, which has become a highly polarized topic since the 2014 shooting of African American man Michael Brown in Ferguson, Missouri.*

"New Study Says White Police Officers Are Not More Likely to Shoot Minority Suspects," by Martin Kaste, NPR, July 26, 2019. Reprinted by permission.

A new peer-reviewed study of fatal police shootings says that white officers are not more likely to shoot and kill minority suspects. Critics contend it doesn't address racial disparities by police.

ARI SHAPIRO, HOST: When you look at the number of police shootings in relation to the population, you find that people of color are shot and killed more often than white people. The reason for that disparity has been intensely debated for years, especially since an unarmed black teenager was shot and killed in Ferguson, Mo., almost five years ago.

There has been one recurring theory, that white cops are more likely to shoot black people because of racial bias. Now a new study is challenging that conclusion. NPR's Martin Kaste has more.

MARTIN KASTE, BYLINE: Since the Ferguson protests of 2014, we've learned a lot more about fatal shootings by the police. News organizations started collecting their own data on shootings to make up for incomplete federal stats, and academics started building on that. Michigan State University psychologist Joseph Cesario is part of a group that looked at fatal shootings in 2015. They added in the race of the police, and then did a statistical analysis.

JOSEPH CESARIO: The race of a police officer did not predict the race of the citizen shot. In other words, black officers were just as likely to shoot black citizens as white officers were.

KASTE: Other studies have looked at this question, but this one comes closest to being a nationwide analysis. It's also getting extra attention because it's in a prestigious peer-reviewed journal, the *Proceedings of the National Academy of Sciences*. And that puzzles Philip Atiba Goff.

PHILIP ATIBA GOFF: I'm a bit surprised that this made its way into PNAS given what they actually found.

KASTE: Goff is a prominent researcher in issues of race and criminal justice and the co-founder of the Center for Policing Equity. He says he applauds the authors for bringing in new data and trying a new approach, but he doesn't think they came up with much.

GOFF: It doesn't do very much to move us towards an understanding of how much are police responsible for racial disparities. And the things it does sort of lead us to are things that we already knew.

KASTE: For instance, he says if the study is aiming to debunk the assumption that white cops shoot people for racist reasons while black cops don't, he says that's a strawman because no one in his field actually thinks that.

GOFF: Racism is not a thing that white people can have and black people can't. And nobody's research would suggest that it does. That's a really wild premise based in no research that no serious scientist should be able to say out loud and then get it published.

KASTE: But the paper's lead author, David J. Johnson of the University of Maryland, says some academics do make that assumption, especially in his field, psychology. And he believes the same assumption is being made by the media.

DAVID J. JOHNSON: I think that you see that in reporting on individual shootings, where they'll mention the race of the officer. And the reason that they mention that is because it's perceived as being relevant. So what we did was, for the first time, tested that assumption.

KASTE: Johnson takes pains to say that this study is not trying to deny the role of race. Instead, what they're trying to do is narrow down where it's having its effect on policing. He says it also raises some questions about a common fix for biased policing, the push to hire more minority officers because if this study is right, just hiring more black cops will not mean fewer black people get shot. And that fits with what implicit bias trainers say.

LORIE FRIDELL: People can have biases against their own demographic groups. Women can have biases about women. Blacks can have biases about blacks. It is incorrect to assume that any issue of bias in policing is brought to us by white males.

KASTE: Lorie Fridell is a criminologist as well as a bias trainer. She says academics have been wrestling with this question for decades, and this latest paper is not about to settle things.

FRIDELL: The defenders of police, of course, will cherry-pick the studies that show no bias. And the other side will cherry-pick the ones that do. But we don't have any definitive studies on this.

KASTE: She thinks people should be more open to the idea that bias and demographics can both play a role. And that's something that the authors of the paper and their critics both seem to agree on.

The real question here is not whether race is a factor in police shootings, but when? Is it beforehand in all the things that might lead up to a shooting, such as drug laws or racial profiling? Or does it come down to the skin color of the individual cop holding the gun?

7

Stop-and-Frisk Data

New York Civil Liberties Union

The New York Civil Liberties Union, founded in 1951, is the New York affiliate of the American Civil Liberties Union. Its mission is to defend and promote the fundamental principles and values embodied in the Bill of Rights, the US Constitution, and the New York Constitution, including freedom of speech and religion, and the right to privacy, equality, and due process of law for all New Yorkers.

The following report shows the tracking of stop-and-frisk police stops and street interrogations in New York City since 2002. At the height of the policy known as stop-and-frisk, in 2011, over 685,000 people were stopped, and research shows that nearly 9 out of 10 stopped-and-frisked New Yorkers were completely innocent. The report shows the inherent racial bias within stop-and-frisk, including how, at most, 12 percent of the people stopped-and-frisked were white, making nearly 90 percent of the stoppages on an annual basis people of color. Additionally, the 2003–2011 data shows that on an annual basis, almost half or more of those stopped were an age group that contains minors, teens, and people in their early twenties.

"Stop-and-Frisk Data," New York Civil Liberties Union, March 4, 2019. Reprinted by permission.

An analysis by the NYCLU revealed that innocent New Yorkers have been subjected to police stops and street interrogations more than 5 million times since 2002, and that Black and Latinx communities continue to be the overwhelming target of these tactics. At the height of stop-and-frisk in 2011 under the Bloomberg administration, over 685,000 people were stopped. Nearly 9 out of 10 stopped-and-frisked New Yorkers have been completely innocent.

According to the NYPD's Annual Reports:

In 2019, 13,459 stops were recorded.

- 8,867 were innocent (66 percent).
- 7,981 were Black (59 percent).
- 3,869 were Latinx (29 percent).
- 1,215 were white (9 percent).

In 2018, 11,008 NYPD stops were recorded.

- 7,645 were innocent (70 percent).
- 6,241 were Black (57 percent).
- 3,389 were Latinx (31 percent).
- 1,074 were white (10 percent).

In 2017, 11,629 NYPD stops were recorded.

- 7,833 were innocent (67 percent).
- 6,595 were Black (57 percent).
- 3,567 were Latinx (31 percent).
- 977 were white (8 percent).

In 2016, 12,404 NYPD stops were recorded.

- 9,394 were innocent (76 percent).
- 6,498 were Black (52 percent).
- 3,626 were Latinx (29 percent).
- 1,270 were white (10 percent).

In 2015, 22,565 NYPD stops were recorded.

- 18,353 were innocent (80 percent).
- 12,223 were Black (54 percent).
- 6,598 were Latinx (29 percent).
- 2,567 were white (11 percent).

In 2014, 45,787 NYPD stops were recorded.

- 37,744 were innocent (82 percent).
- 24,319 were Black (53 percent).
- 12,489 were Latinx (27 percent).
- 5,467 were white (12 percent).

In 2013, 191,851 NYPD stops were recorded.

- 169,252 were innocent (88 percent).
- 104,958 were Black (56 percent).
- 55,191 were Latinx (29 percent).
- 20,877 were white (11 percent).

In 2012, 532,911 NYPD stops were recorded.

- 473,644 were innocent (89 percent).
- 284,229 were Black (55 percent).
- 165,140 were Latinx (32 percent).
- 50,366 were white (10 percent).

In 2011, 685,724 NYPD stops were recorded.

- 605,328 were innocent (88 percent).
- 350,743 were Black (53 percent).
- 223,740 were Latinx (34 percent).
- 61,805 were white (9 percent).
- 341,581 were aged 14–24 (51 percent).

In 2010, 601,285 NYPD stops were recorded.

- 518,849 were innocent (86 percent).

- 315,083 were Black (54 percent).
- 189,326 were Latinx (33 percent).
- 54,810 were white (9 percent).
- 295,902 were aged 14–24 (49 percent).

In 2009, 581,168 NYPD stops were recorded.

- 510,742 were innocent (88 percent).
- 310,611 were Black (55 percent).
- 180,055 were Latinx (32 percent).
- 53,601 were white (10 percent).
- 289,602 were aged 14–24 (50 percent).

In 2008, 540,302 NYPD stops were recorded.

- 474,387 were innocent (88 percent).
- 275,588 were Black (53 percent).
- 168,475 were Latinx (32 percent).
- 57,650 were white (11 percent).
- 263,408 were aged 14–24 (49 percent).

In 2007, 472,096 NYPD stops were recorded.

- 410,936 were innocent (87 percent).
- 243,766 were Black (54 percent).
- 141,868 were Latinx (31 percent).
- 52,887 were white (12 percent).
- 223,783 were aged 14–24 (48 percent).

In 2006, 506,491 NYPD stops were recorded.

- 457,163 were innocent (90 percent).
- 267,468 were Black (53 percent).
- 147,862 were Latinx (29 percent).
- 53,500 were white (11 percent).
- 247,691 were aged 14–24 (50 percent).

In 2005, 398,191 NYPD stops were recorded.

- 352,348 were innocent (89 percent).
- 196,570 were Black (54 percent).
- 115,088 were Latinx (32 percent).
- 40,713 were white (11 percent).
- 189,854 were aged 14–24 (51 percent).

In 2004, 313,523 NYPD stops were recorded.

- 278,933 were innocent (89 percent).
- 155,033 were Black (55 percent).
- 89,937 were Latinx (32 percent).
- 28,913 were white (10 percent).
- 152,196 were aged 14–24 (52 percent).

In 2003, 160,851 NYPD stops were recorded.

- 140,442 were innocent (87 percent).
- 77,704 were Black (54 percent).
- 44,581 were Latinx (31 percent).
- 17,623 were white (12 percent).
- 83,499 were aged 14–24 (55 percent).

In 2002, 97,296 NYPD stops were recorded.

- 80,176 were innocent (82 percent).

NYCLU's most recent detailed analysis of stop-and-frisk data and practices can be found in our 2019 report, "Stop-and-Frisk in the de Blasio Era."

About the Data

Every time a police officer stops a person in NYC, the officer is supposed to fill out a form recording the details of the stop. The forms were filled out by hand and manually entered into an NYPD database until 2017, when the forms became electronic. The NYPD reports stop-and-frisk data in two ways: a summary report released quarterly and a complete database released annually to the public.

The quarterly reports are released by the NYCLU every three months and include data on stops, arrests, and summonses. The data are broken down by precinct of the stop and race and gender of the person stopped.

The annual database includes nearly all of the data recorded by the police officer after a stop, such as the age of the person stopped, if a person was frisked, if there was a weapon or firearm recovered, if physical force was used, and the exact location of the stop within the precinct. The NYPD uploads this data to their website annually.

8

If Overpolicing Happened to Everyone

Sarah A. Seo

Sarah A. Seo is a legal historian of criminal law and procedure in the twentieth-century United States at the University of Iowa College of Law. She is the author of Policing the Open Road: How Cars Transformed American Freedom *(Harvard University Press, 2019), which examines the history of the automobile to explain the evolution of Fourth Amendment jurisprudence and to explore the problem of police discretion in a society committed to the rule of law. Seo has also been published in the* Yale Law Journal, Law and Social Inquiry, *and* Law and History Review, *among others.*

In the following viewpoint, Sarah A. Seo of the Cato Institute explores the shift in American policing before and after the expanded rollout of cars through her book, Policing the Open Road. *Prior to the mass production of cars, police officers disciplined drunks and vagrants, but everyone else was self-regulated through common law and voluntary associations. In the 1920s amid the ubiquity of cars—a majority of families had one by this time—self-regulation was rendered inadequate. The author also explores the evolution of policing to the concept of "Driving While Black" and the problem of overpolicing and too many laws regarding drivers in cars.*

"If Overpolicing Happened to Everyone," by Sarah A. Seo, Cato Institute, April 19, 2019. Reprinted by permission.

I am grateful for the thought-provoking responses from Clark Neily, Lars Trautman, and John Pfaff. It is a privilege for a historian to engage with experts working on real-world issues, so I've been looking forward to this conversation.

A common theme in the three response essays is the surprise of reading a history of criminal justice from the perspective of Everyman, or the "law-abiding citizen." While there are many unexpected turns in this history, one aspect that may not be too surprising is that when government officials were dealing with respectable folks, the punitive instinct took time to develop.

Policing was not a widespread mode of governing American society before cars. True, police officers disciplined drunks and vagrants. But everybody else was self-regulated through the common law and voluntary associations like churches and trade unions. Chapter 1 of my book *Policing the Open Road* describes the strange, sometimes comical, attempts to persuade citizen-drivers to follow the rules of the road by appealing to their honor and reasonableness.

Only after officials and policymakers resigned themselves to the fact that such appeals were insufficient did they supplement traffic law enforcement with criminal punishment. It was the incorrigibility of law-abiding citizens that made the punitive response necessary as a last-resort. Because so many people drove—a majority of families had a car by the mid-1920s—and because every town and city in the country had to deal with the sudden ubiquity of cars, the automobile rendered nineteenth-century self-regulation inadequate and ushered in twentieth-century police governance.

Just how much of this shift was about cars? And, as Lars Trautman asks, where does the practice of stop-and-frisk fit into this story? Even before cars, the police harassed people if they looked out of place. But cars completely changed the historical trajectory of this practice in two ways.

First, traffic policing led to much more policing generally. To use Los Angeles as an example, between 1902 and 1912, the ratio of patrolmen to residents increased by a third. During the same period, traffic arrests went up by over twentyfold, and order-maintenance types of offenses (begging, drunkenness, disturbing the peace, and vagrancy) increased by 45 percent.

Confirming the causation between cars and routine policing, the Los Angeles Police Department reported in 1912 that while the largest task of the traffic squad—which they discovered was "practically self-supporting" from the fines it collected—was to direct traffic, it also "assisted in the general work of the Police Department." In other words, the need to manage traffic led to more police officers, who then were able to do more police work.

Second, although cars did not precede the existence of police discretion, the policing of "law-abiding" lawbreakers did make it visible as a legal issue. Consider this counterfactual: what would the history of stop-and-frisks look like if the police did not bother respectable people? I submit that the practice would have stayed under the radar.

Here's why: *Terry v. Ohio* was decided in 1968, which came pretty late in the social and legal history of stop-and-frisks. Back in the 1930s and 40s, progressive legal reformers had tried to legalize stop-and-frisks. Under the common law, stop-and-frisks were illegal without a valid arrest based on probable cause. The unlawful practice had not been controversial and rarely received the attention of judges and law professors—until cops began to stop and frisk respectable people. Reformers believed that legalization would allay any hard feelings that an innocent person might harbor, while also allowing the police to continue stopping and frisking criminal suspects.

Ultimately, the *Terry* rule adopted the earlier proposals; the opinion even cited them. The Warren Court attempted to strike a balance between individual rights and law enforcement needs by requiring reasonable suspicion. It was a lower standard than probable cause, but at least it was more than mere suspicion, the standard that the state of Ohio had sought.

To create an entirely new category of searches and seizures that did not require probable cause, both Chief Justice Warren and the earlier reformers cited *Carroll v. United States*. That's right—the 1925 case that established the automobile exception, and the very first time that the Court created a new category of searches and seizures that did not require warrants.

Chapter 3 of *Policing the Open Road* tells the history from *Carroll* to *Terry* in more detail. The point that I want to emphasize here is to confirm Trautman's observation that the "same courts falling over themselves to find all manner of traffic related actions 'reasonable' and therefore sufficient to support a stop have done the same sort of mental gymnastics to uphold all manner of stop-and-frisk situations."

I would go even further to say that cases on the police's authority to stop and search a person or a car were mutually reinforcing. *Carroll* provided precedent for *Terry*, which, in turn, provided precedent for later car cases. In fact, the first case to "give some flesh to the bones of *Terry*" involved the frisk of a person sitting in a parked car. In the car-dominated United States, the law on policing cars specifically, and the law on policing generally, built on each other.

Policing the Open Road explains how the history of policing Every Driver ended with Driving While Black. Neily's criticism of *Whren v. United States* is not only spot-on, it describes the problem more incisively than my initial essay suggests. It's troubling that under the Supreme Court's interpretation, the Fourth Amendment countenances pretextual policing and racial profiling. So what is surprising is that the decision was unanimous. What explains the Supreme Court's consensus on this injustice?

The *Whren* opinion itself eliminated one possible explanation. Before *Whren* was decided, several lower courts had cited the challenges of proving that an officer had ulterior motives for stopping a car. But the Court specifically disclaimed evidentiary difficulties as a basis for its ruling.

I suspect that the answer lies in a concern that "traffic law exceptionalism" could end up undermining the rule of law.

As Justice O'Connor remarked, "I don't know of any other area" of law where "sooner or later most of us are going to commit some traffic violation." If everybody violates the traffic code, then its enforcement must, by necessity, be selective. This may seem troubling. But selective enforcement alone does not pose a constitutional problem. Police agencies have to prioritize which laws to enforce because of the reality that their resources are limited.

Whren's lawyer argued, however, that traffic laws are "unique." There are so many rules and regulations that police officers effectively exercise unrestrained discretion, the very definition of arbitrary power.

But if the Court were to permit a criminal defendant to claim a Fourth Amendment violation based on a pretextual speeding ticket, then a driver could challenge a valid speeding ticket based on pretext—a scenario that several justices mentioned during oral argument. The resulting state of affairs would wreak havoc on traffic-law enforcement and public safety on the streets and highways.

And although traffic laws seem special in how normal and frequent violations are, traffic lawbreaking is arguably an extreme example of a common phenomenon in the modern United States. There are many laws, rules, and regulations that are routinely ignored by both citizens and their enforcers.

The problem, then, is determining "at what point a code of law becomes so expansive and so commonly violated that infraction itself can no longer be the ordinary measure of the lawfulness of enforcement," as the *Whren* opinion put it. Today the challenge might involve traffic laws, but the next case might be about the Clean Water Act, and so on. And if the Court were to get in the business of reviewing when valid laws are effectively repealed by widespread lawbreaking—to the point of punishing the police for enforcing those laws—then the rule of law would be turned upside-down.

But what is different about traffic laws from, say, the Clean Water Act, is the racial tilt of criminal patrol. One way of drawing the line between lawful and unlawful enforcement of the laws that everyone violates is to maintain that racially discriminatory enforcement is unconstitutional. This was precisely Whren's argument, which the Court rejected—at least under the Fourth Amendment. According to *Whren*, claims of unequal enforcement must be brought under the Fourteenth Amendment's Equal Protection Clause.

This seems fair enough, and perhaps even the liberal justices signed on to *Whren* because minority defendants may at least have an equal protection claim.

But there are still two reasons to rue the Court's decision. First, the very same year that it decided *Whren*, the Court also decided *United States v. Armstrong*, which set forth what criminal defendants must do when trying to make a selective prosecution claim on the basis of race. To put it simply, *Armstrong* made it nearly impossible to do so.

Second, whether one thinks about the overpolicing of minorities as a Fourth Amendment issue or an equal protection issue makes a difference. Viewing this primarily as a discrimination problem, rather than as a problem of policing itself, obscures an important normative question about how much power the police should have in a free and democratic society. Should the police be able to search a car during a routine traffic stop? Should it be possible for minor traffic violations to lead to an unrelated criminal investigation? Unfortunately, these are not the questions that are asked when arguing that minority Americans are not treated the same as "Everyman."

Finally, John Pfaff ended his response essay with the troubling thought that police reform may face an uphill battle because "when people otherwise uninvolved with the criminal justice system hear about police brutality, aggressiveness, and harassment, they have personal experiences to turn to—experiences that do not line up with those accounts." I agree wholeheartedly that this is a hurdle. My hope for *Policing the Open Road* is that readers will never stop asking how our policies and laws would change if the overpolicing of cars happened to us all.

9

When Cops Misbehave, Who Has the Right to Know?

Abbie VanSickle

Abbie VanSickle covers criminal justice in California for the Marshall Project. She has worked as a reporter for the University of California, Berkeley Investigative Reporting Program, the Center for Investigative Reporting, and the Tampa Bay Times. *Her work has appeared in the* New York Times, *the* Washington Post, *and the* Los Angeles Times. *She is a graduate of the UC Berkeley School of Law and a lecturer at its Graduate School of Journalism. From 2011 to 2012, she was a Henry Luce Scholar in Cambodia, where she worked on behalf of survivors at the Khmer Rouge Tribunal.*

In the following viewpoint, Abbie VanSickle explores how California has some of the strictest laws regarding prosecutors' access to police officer personnel files. Because of US Supreme Court Case Brady v. Maryland, *prosecutors have a duty to turn over any evidence favorable to the accused, including records of police misconduct. The author explores the workarounds made by law enforcement and prosecutors in San Francisco, and how a 2015 case that reached the California Supreme Court argued the need for a clear system to allow prosecutors and defense lawyers to find out about police misconduct.*

"When Cops Misbehave, Who Has the Right to Know," by Abbie VanSickle, The Marshall Project, February 13, 2019. Reprinted by permission.

When Jerry Coleman heard about a domestic violence prosecution winding its way through San Francisco's criminal courts, he knew he'd finally found his test case.

In November 2012, San Francisco police officers arrested 20-year-old Daryl Lee Johnson, accusing him of hitting his girlfriend and grabbing her phone during an argument so she couldn't call police, according to court records. (In California "injuring a wireless communications device" is a misdemeanor.)

Because Johnson's girlfriend refused to testify, the only witnesses were two San Francisco police officers. Both officers had long records of misconduct. In the past two years, courts had held 24 hearings on material tucked away in the officers' files. In each, a judge had ruled records must be turned over. All together, there were 505 pages of records in the two officers' files that courts determined could be favorable for a defendant.

"We knew there was dirt, and we knew it was relevant, we just didn't know what it was," said Coleman, who then worked as a supervisor in the San Francisco District Attorney's Office.

It may come as a surprise to learn that California, despite its liberal reputation, goes farther than nearly any other state at shielding records of police misconduct. Although other states make police records confidential, California is the only state that clearly bars prosecutors from reviewing entire police personnel files.

Johnson was ultimately convicted of vandalism and sentenced to the 10 days he had served, but his case led to a lawsuit that could determine whether prosecutors have access—and how much—to records of law enforcement misconduct. That lawsuit, along with legislative efforts to crack open the records, may transform California from one of the least into one of the nation's most open states for police records.

In 2015, Johnson's case reached the California Supreme Court. There, the justices examined a system created by the San Francisco District Attorney's Office and the police department aimed at giving prosecutors notice when officers had serious misconduct charges, while also complying with California's strict police protection law.

Under a famous Supreme Court case called *Brady v. Maryland*, prosecutors have a duty to turn over any evidence favorable to the accused, including misconduct by police. But in California, that's tricky since prosecutors aren't allowed to see police personnel files, thanks to legislation passed in the late 1970s at the behest of the state's law enforcement unions.

In San Francisco, the prosecutors and police had devised a workaround—a police committee reviewed records and turned over the names of officers with records of disciplinary problems if those officers were witnesses in particular cases. Prosecutors then asked judges to review the officers' records and give them anything relevant.

They ran into a hitch when the judge in Johnson's case refused to review records, telling prosecutors he considered that type of work suited for paralegals, not judges. Prosecutors took the case all the way to the California Supreme Court in 2015, arguing that there needed to be a clear system to allow prosecutors and defense lawyers to find out about police misconduct.

"We thought that (Johnson's case) would trigger a lot more law enforcement agencies to do what we did, and the L.A. sheriff was doing just that," said Coleman, who is now retired and working as an adjunct law professor at the University of San Francisco.

A subsequent opinion by then-Attorney General Kamala Harris appeared to bolster San Francisco's model, and it spread throughout the state, including to the Los Angeles County Sheriff's Department, one of the state's largest policing agencies. The Sheriff's Department compiled a list of about 300 deputies with histories of misconduct. When the sheriff announced the policy, he referred to the Supreme Court's decision in the Johnson case. But when the sheriff said he planned to share those names with prosecutors, a union for the deputies sued, arguing that the disclosure law violates their right to privacy.

The case has roiled the legal community, particularly after the *Los Angeles Times* published descriptions of the misconduct by deputies, which they estimated could taint 62,000 felony cases. One deputy had planted evidence by using taco sauce as fake blood. Another deputy shot pepper-spray into an elderly man's face and then wrote a false report about the incident to justify arresting him.

It comes at a time when there is increasing support in the legislature to unravel some of the 1970s laws that shield records of police misconduct from public view.

Last spring, the fatal police shooting of Stephon Clark, who was unarmed when Sacramento police shot him in his grandmother's backyard while investigating a complaint that someone was breaking car windows, ignited protests and led to a law known as "SB 1421." The new law makes four categories of police records open to the public: incidents of sexual assault by on-duty officers, records of lying by officers in court or in reports, reports in police shootings and reports about use of force that leads to serious injury or death.

"[The bill] lifted a veil of secrecy that existed in California for 40 years on almost any and every record of law enforcement," said Sen. Nancy Skinner, a Democrat from Berkeley, the author of the bill. "It doesn't cover all conduct, but it does cover what prosecutors and the public most deserve to have access to."

Like the decision to turn over deputies' names in Los Angeles, Skinner's bill has already drawn protest from law enforcement. Just as the law went into effect, a group of law enforcement unions asked the California Supreme Court to block the release of any records created before Jan. 1, 2019. The court denied the request.

In early January, the state Supreme Court asked the parties to answer how the new law would affect the L.A. sheriff's case.

Only the California District Attorneys Association has weighed in so far, arguing that the new law shows an increased public awareness and support for more access to records long kept hidden from view.

The court is not the only place this dispute is playing out. At least one city, Inglewood, in southwestern Los Angeles County, has faced accusations of trying to thwart the new law. In the weeks before the new law went into effect, city officials authorized police to shred records from more than 100 police shootings and other internal investigation reports. The city has a history of controversial police shootings and was the subject of a 2009 Department of Justice investigation that was critical of the police department's use-of-force policies.

After civil rights advocates raised questions, city officials said it was merely a routine clearing of old files no longer needed by the police department.

10

Policing in Black and White

Kirsten Weir

Kirsten Weir's work has appeared in newspapers, magazines, websites, and books, including publications such as Discover, New Scientist, Popular Science, Psychology Today, Nautilus, *and* Scientific American Mind. *In addition to writing for national consumer magazines, she has created content for trade magazines, custom publications, and websites. She is a senior writer for the content marketing agency Aha Media and a contributing writer for the* Monitor on Psychology, *the monthly magazine of the American Psychological Association.*

In the following viewpoint, Kirsten Weir discusses the implicit biases in policing and chronicles the shift the science behind it has made from solely existing in research to the forefront of national media. Racial bias was a significant topic during the 2016 US presidential campaign and has only become more prevalent in 2020. The author also highlights that many of the biases faced by people—not just the police—are subconscious biases, though with the police come life-altering implications. Weir showcases that with 15,000 law enforcement agencies in the United States, it is challenging to pinpoint exactly what it means to have a significant bias against Black Americans. At the same time, many studies highlighted in the viewpoint show that there is evidence of biases against Black Americans in law enforcement.

"Policing in Black & White," by Kirsten Weir, American Psychological Association, December 2016. Reprinted by permission.

Do you believe police are implicitly biased against black people?" When NBC newsman Lester Holt asked Hillary Clinton this question in the first presidential debate, it was a sure sign the science of implicit bias had jumped from the psychology journals into the public consciousness—and that racial bias in law enforcement has entered the national dialogue.

There's evidence of racial disparities at many levels of law enforcement, from traffic stops to drug-related arrests to use of force. But the roots of those disparities aren't always clear. Experts point to systemic problems as well as the implicit (largely unconscious) biases mentioned in the debate. To be sure, those biases aren't unique to police. But in matters of criminal justice, implicit bias can have life-altering implications.

Social media has turned a spotlight on cases of racial discrimination. As the list of black citizens killed by nonblack officers grows, tensions between black communities and police are running high. "It's a nuanced problem but people continue to take a polarized view," says Jack Glaser, PhD, a social psychologist at the University of California, Berkeley. "It's not productive to demonize police."

Glaser says police departments are eager for solutions that will reduce racial disparities. "Police chiefs know what the stakes are," he says. Policymakers, too, are keen to take action. In October, for instance, the New Jersey attorney general issued a directive requiring mandatory classes in racial bias for police officers in the state. Psychologists, meanwhile, have the skills to understand discrimination and point to evidence-based solutions. "This is an area that's worth a lot of investment in research, and important for psychologists to think about," Glaser says.

Evidence of Inequality

With more than 15,000 law enforcement agencies across the country operating at the federal, state and local levels, there is no "typical" police department. Still, evidence for racial disparities is growing. Most of those data focus on the treatment of black civilians by white officers. In an analysis of national police-shootings data from 2011–14, for example, Cody T. Ross, a doctoral student in anthropology at the University of California, Davis, concluded there is "evidence of a significant bias in the killing of unarmed black Americans relative to unarmed white Americans." The probability of being black, unarmed and shot by police is about 3.5 times the probability of being white, unarmed and shot by police, he found (*PLOS One*, 2015).

Other studies conflict with that finding. Harvard University economist Roland G. Fryer Jr., PhD, examined more than 1,000 shootings in 10 major police departments and found no racial differences in officer-involved shootings. Fryer did, however, find that black civilians are more likely to experience other types of force, including being handcuffed without arrest, pepper-sprayed or pushed to the ground by an officer (National Bureau of Economic Research, 2016).

Those disparities don't seem to arise from the fact that black Americans are more likely to commit crimes. Supporting this point is research by Phillip Atiba Goff, PhD, a social psychologist at the University of California, Los Angeles, co-founder of the Center for Policing Equity. Goff, Glaser and colleagues reviewed data from 12 police departments and found that black residents were more often subjected to police force than white residents, even after adjusting for whether the person had been arrested for violent crimes (Center for Policing Equity, 2016).

Other data show that black people are also more likely to be stopped by police. Stanford University social psychologist Jennifer Eberhardt, PhD, and colleagues analyzed data from the police department in Oakland, California, and found that while black residents make up 28 percent of the Oakland population, they accounted for 60 percent of police stops. What's more, black men were four times more likely than white men to be searched during a traffic stop, even though officers were no more likely to recover contraband when searching black suspects (Stanford SPARQ, 2016).

And in Falcon Heights, Minnesota, where cafeteria worker Philando Castile was fatally shot by a nonblack officer in July after being pulled over for a broken taillight, statistics released by the local St. Anthony Police Department showed that about 7 percent of residents in the area are black, but they account for 47 percent of arrests.

The Police Officer's Dilemma

Many factors can account for the differences in treatment at the hands of police. In some jurisdictions, explicit prejudice still occurs, says John Dovidio, PhD, a social psychologist at Yale University who studies both implicit and explicit prejudice. Many police departments and officers take a paramilitary approach to law and order, and sometimes adopt an "us-versus-them" attitude toward black communities, he says. "There can be a lot of dehumanization that occurs in the conversations people have, and that's explicit."

In many cases, however, the biases come from unconscious or unintentional beliefs. "A large proportion of white Americans have these [implicit] biases, and it's hard to expect police officers to be any different," Dovidio says.

Implicit biases are attitudes or stereotypes that can influence our beliefs, actions and decisions, even though we're not consciously aware of them and don't express those beliefs verbally to ourselves or others. One of the most well-demonstrated types of implicit bias is the unconscious association between black individuals and crime. That association can influence an officer's behavior, even if he or she doesn't hold or express explicitly racist beliefs.

Goff describes implicit bias as a kind of identity trap. "They're situations that trap us into behaving in ways that are not consistent with our values," he says.

Joshua Correll, PhD, a psychologist at the University of Colorado, has explored one facet of implicit racial bias in a series of laboratory studies since 2000. He developed and tested a paradigm known as "the police officer's dilemma," using a first-person-shooter video game. Participants are presented with images of young men, white and black, holding either guns or innocuous objects such as cellphones or soda cans. The goal is to shoot armed targets but not unarmed targets.

The researchers found that participants shoot armed targets more often and more quickly if they're black rather than white, and refrain from shooting more often when the target is white. The most common mistakes are shooting an unarmed black target and failing to shoot an armed white target (*Journal of Personality and Social Psychology*, 2002).

But experiments with police officers show a more complex pattern. Similar to community participants, officers showed evidence of bias in their reaction times, more quickly reacting to armed black targets and unarmed white targets—in other words, targets that aligned with racial stereotypes. But those biases evident in their reaction times did not translate to their ultimate decision to shoot or not shoot (*Journal of Personality and Social Psychology*, 2007). Still, that's only part of the story. In later work, Correll found special unit officers who regularly interact with minority gang members were more likely to exhibit racial bias in their decision to shoot. When officers' training and experiences confirm racial stereotypes, those biases appear to hold more sway over their behavior (*Personality and Social Psychology Bulletin*, 2013).

Bad Habits

While research points to some patterns in implicit bias, we still have a lot to learn about the ways that biases influence people's decisions and behavior in the real world, says David M. Corey, PhD, a police psychologist and founding president of the American Board of Police and Public Safety Psychology. "Yes, implicit bias can affect us. The more important questions are, which persons are affected, and under what conditions?"

Yet while those questions remain unanswered, many police departments and policymakers have skipped ahead to a different one: What can be done to reduce implicit bias? "The police officers I've worked with are looking for effective ways to reduce implicit or unintended bias, and they welcome advice based on psychological evidence, not politics," says Corey.

Under pressure from the public, many police departments have implemented implicit bias workshops and trainings. That could be premature, says Corey. "We feel like we have to do something, but sometimes the action we take proves to be merely window dressing," he says. "My worry is that could cause a police agency to think they're doing enough, or that the monies being spent will prohibit spending for other areas, including research."

That hasn't stopped some departments from moving forward, however—a step that concerns Glaser and others who think evidence should come before implementation. "There are contractors that provide [implicit bias training], but there's zero evidence that what they do has an impact," Glaser says. "We don't know how to lastingly change implicit biases, particularly those as robust and prevalent as race and crime—and not for lack of trying."

Recently, psychologist Calvin K. Lai, PhD, at Harvard University, and colleagues tested nine different interventions designed to reduce implicit racial biases. Some interventions aimed to introduce participants to exemplary individuals that ran counter to traditional stereotypes, for example. Other strategies included priming participants to consider multicultural attitudes, or teaching participants strategies to create implementation intentions (such as repeating to themselves, "If I see a black face, I will respond by thinking 'good.'"). In two studies with more than 6,300 participants, all of the interventions reduced implicit prejudice in the short term. But none of those changes lasted more than a couple of days following the intervention—and in some cases, the effects vanished within a few hours (*Journal of Experimental Psychology*, 2016). "Implicit associations are habits of mind," Dovidio says. "And habits are really hard to change."

That's not to say there's no value in training officers. But rather than trying to eliminate their unintentional biases, it might be more fruitful to stack the deck so that officers are less likely to act on those biases. "Character is a weak predictor of behavior, but situations are strong predictors of behaviors," Goff says. And changing situations can be more feasible than changing ingrained stereotypes.

Imagine, for example, officers chasing a perpetrator after a crime has occurred. "As they chase the person, it's building up their adrenaline. All of the biases they have come together like a perfect storm," Dovidio says—a storm that can lead to excessive force. To circumvent that possibility, he says, some police departments have implemented a policy that the officer who chases a suspect should not be the one to initiate subsequent steps, such as booking the suspect or leading the interrogation. "You try to build in structures and procedures that help overcome the tendencies," he explains.

Creating protocols and checklists for various law-enforcement situations can also help remove bias from the equation, adds Tom Tyler, PhD, a professor of law and psychology at Yale Law School. Federal authorities, for example, use such checklists when deciding whether to search airline travelers for drugs: Did the person use an alias? Did they pay for their tickets with cash? Are they using evasive movements? So far, checklists haven't been rolled out for everyday street stops, Tyler says, though such protocols could help reduce bias when officers decide whether to search a suspect or pull over a driver. "In ambiguous situations, people are more likely to act on bias," Tyler says. "If you have a script to follow, that's more objective."

Implementing protocols to circumvent bias could be helpful in the short term. Looking ahead, changing hiring practices could be an effective way to reduce racial disparities, says Corey, whose research focuses on selecting new officers. His research explores the cognitive characteristics that make a person more likely to resist the automatic effects of implicit bias.

For example, he points to research by B. Keith Payne, PhD, at Ohio State University, who found that people with poor executive control were more likely to express automatic race biases as behavior discrimination (*Journal of Personality and Social Psychology*, 2005). By hiring police candidates who already possess qualities such as greater executive control, Corey says, "we can select police officers less likely to require cognitive reshaping."

Rebuilding Community

Reducing and circumventing bias is one way to chip away at the disparities in how police treat black civilians. Another is to focus on the positive. Many departments are taking a fresh look at community policing, in which police and community members collaborate to rebuild trust and build safer neighborhoods.

Experts say efforts to reach across racial lines to build ties with community members could help to reduce disparities. Community policing efforts might include town meetings, polls and surveys, sitting down with interest groups and foot patrols to increase an officer's interactions with the neighborhood.

It's hardly a radical concept. "In the past, an officer used to walk a beat. They'd get out of their car, get to know people," says Dovidio. "When you don't have those personal experiences, you tend to treat people in a homogeneous way."

But over the last several decades that policing style has fallen out of favor as police have taken a hard line on minor offenses in an effort to reduce crime rates. "Policing in last 30 years in America has focused on a mission of crime control," says Tyler. Departments began adopting procedures such as New York City's controversial "stop-and-frisk" program, which encouraged officers to stop pedestrians and search them for weapons and contraband. Columbia University statistician Andrew Gelman, PhD, and colleagues reported that the program had the effect of disproportionately targeting black and Hispanic citizens, even after controlling for race-specific crime rates in the various precincts (*Journal of the American Statistical Association*, 2007).

Critics say such programs drive a wedge between police and community members, eroding trust. That lack of trust could be particularly problematic when layered on top of implicit racial stereotypes. "Effective policing requires the cooperation of the community. If the community doesn't trust you, they won't give you info to help you do your job," says Dovidio. "If you can create a sense of being on the same team, having the same goals, it makes policing more effective."

Writing on the Wall

As citizens continue to demand change, police departments increasingly understand the importance of taking action, says Tyler. "I think many see the writing on the wall. It's in their interest to get ahead of the curve to prepare and reduce the likelihood of these politically damaging events."

Major police departments such as Chicago and New York City are making efforts to take action based on evidence, he says. And the Department of Justice recently issued a final report from the President's Task Force on 21st Century Policing that drew from research including the psychological literature, he says. "On the highest level, national leaders in policing are making an effort to do things based in research," Tyler says.

As such efforts continue, psychologists can help by studying disparities, developing new interventions and testing what works in the real world.

Glaser, for instance, is a co-investigator on the National Justice Database, a project at the Center for Policing Equity with funding from the National Science Foundation. The project team is studying use-of-force data to identify the variations in policies, practices and culture that could predict excessive force. "Data analysis doesn't solve problems on its own, but it helps to point to solutions," he says.

Dovidio adds that to be most effective, psychologists might take a hard look at their preconceived ideas about law enforcement. "If more psychologists understood how policing operates and the challenges that police face, we could do a lot in terms of creating partnerships for effective training and applications of psychological theory," he says.

11

Going Above and Beyond the Call of Duty

Emily Alvarenga

Emily Alvarenga covers features and business for the Signal. *She graduated from San Diego State University in 2017 and has been writing and reporting since she was a high school student.*

In the following viewpoint, Emily Alvarenga chronicles the journey of a local man named Captain Rick Godinez to becoming a firefighter, from starting at the Fire Academy as the youngest in his class to being one of the pioneers for Urban Search and Rescue (USAR). Godinez has seen deployments through a number of notable local incidents in the Los Angeles area, including the tumultuous 1992 Los Angeles riots and the aftermath of the terror attacks in New York City on September 11, 2001. Today, Godinez continues to give back to the community, serving as a captain in the public information office of the Los Angeles Fire Department.

"Going Above and Beyond the Call of Duty," by Emily Alvarenga, *The Santa Clarita Valley Signal*, February 5, 2020. Reprinted by permission.

In his 36 years as a firefighter, Capt. II Rick Godinez has seen it all—from natural disasters to the aftermath of the 9/11 terrorist attacks.

From his roles as a firefighter to fire chaplain, public information officer to incident support team member, the Santa Clarita resident has gone above and beyond the call of duty while with the Los Angeles Fire Department, according to his peers.

And now, as Godinez enters his final days before retirement, he's about to get the cherry on top: the distinguished award for Firefighter of the Year.

"Never in my wildest dreams did I think I was going to get to do half of the stuff (I've done)," he said.

A Call to Action

Godinez remembers being a freshman in high school when he was told he should know what he wants to be by the end of the 10th grade.

"It's kind of ridiculous to think about," he said. "What high school sophomore knows what he wants to do? But it just was in the back of my mind."

After visiting LAFD Station 87, which was right down the street from his house, with his brother and watching several episodes of "Emergency," Godinez decided he had found his calling.

"My junior year, I went back to the station and talked to the firefighters there, and I was convinced… I really wanted to be a firefighter," he said. "From that point on, for the next two years, that was what I was going to pursue."

Though it took a few years, Godinez remained committed to his goal, working toward an associate degree in fire science while training as a fire explorer.

"I was just focused on this was going to happen—this was like do or die," he said, laughing. "And, it was my dream job."

That dedication paid off, and a week after his 21st birthday, he started the Fire Academy as the youngest in his class.

Some of the Notable Incidents

"I was told really early in my career that I needed to become a subject matter expert at something, whatever it might be, and for me, it was urban search and rescue and public information officer," he added.

After being one of the pioneers for USAR in L.A., his department began teaching other agencies.

"We flew to San Francisco for this one-day operation … and it was all to see if we can get our personnel and equipment onto a C-130 and fly out within a certain period of time," he said. "From that training and that event, (we) became California Task Force 1, which is one of 28 teams nationally that go out the door for earthquakes, hurricanes, disasters. So, I've been on that team since the inception."

That has led to a plethora of memorable experiences, such as deploying to a number of hurricanes and to Haiti after the 2010 earthquake, as well as quite a few notable local incidents, like the 1992 L.A. riots and 1994 Northridge earthquake.

One of those instances Godinez said he'll never forget was his deployment to New York after 9/11.

"9/11 was its own, very surreal (experience), and what made that unique in its own sense was the fact that we knew … we're going to go through this rubble pile and there's going to be firefighters in there," he said.

For the first time, a critical incident stress team was deployed, not to search as there were others who had already been sent to do so, but to help firefighters get through it all.

"The site, the smell, the visuals were just—it's just really unbelievable," he said. "When you picture 210-story buildings, reduced to just maybe five, six stories high of rubble. And, the unique thing was there was nothing recognizable. It wasn't office chairs, toilets, phones … everything was pulverized, so it was just this smoldering pile of metal and debris."

He remembers standing over the pile, talking with a New York fire lieutenant, who was waiting for the OK to continue searching, when the firefighter started to cry.

"I mean, tears are flowing down his eyes, and I go, 'You OK?'" Godinez said. "And he goes, 'My two boys are in that pile.' And he had two sons—one was a police officer and one was a firefighter... I had no words."

At that moment, they were approached by another firefighter who handed them each a pile of letters.

"They were just handwritten drawings and letters, (that said), 'Dear firefighter, you're my hero, thank you,'" he said, adding that there was not a dry eye around as each first responder dug into their pile. "It was the perfect moment, because this guy, he needed that."

Giving Back

In his spare time, Godinez has also traveled on numerous mission trips with Firefighters for Christ and other organizations, either to build something or to train the local fire departments.

"We teach them firefighting skills, brush fire fighting skills, and some low, high angle rescues, sometimes swift water rescue skills," he said. "It's about a week-long training. We go on our own dime, and we bring (them) a lot of tools and equipment."

Years ago, Godinez also put that faith into action for his own as he took on the role of fire chaplain.

Though voluntary, senior fire chaplains are available 24 hours a day, seven days a week, and perform invocations at various ceremonies, such as memorials, weddings, hospital visits, graduations and line-of-duty death ceremonies.

"It totally took me out of my comfort zone, but it was a good thing," he said. "I think we reached a lot of people, helped a lot of people, during that very critical, vulnerable time in their life."

Among his many other volunteer efforts, Godinez is also a board member of the Los Angeles Firemen's Relief Association, a nonprofit dedicated to helping firefighters and their families, and is the founder of the Family Support Group, which unifies the more than 800 widows with retired and active firefighters in their time of need.

"So, when a firefighter dies, whether it's on duty or not, we're still there for the families," he said. "I love this organization, (and I'm) very passionate about it."

Godinez said he plans to continue working with the organization into retirement, as well as continuing with his duties as a chaplain.

The Nomination

William Wick, a captain II at LAFD, has worked with Godinez for about 20 years and was the one who brought him on as a captain in the public information office.

"In a short amount of time, (Godinez) excelled at his job, not only because of his likable personality, but his ability to communicate in a factual and engaging way," Wick said, adding that Godinez always kept a cool demeanor on difficult calls. "I may have a higher rank, but believe me, in all regards he was definitely the senior member and leader of our station … and he was my true leader."

Though normally Wick doesn't go out of his way to recognize his colleagues, he said he felt it was an obligation and a duty to nominate Godinez for Firefighter of the Year.

"He asked me not to do it out of humbleness, but I don't really listen to him anyway," Wick added, chuckling. "(Godinez) was in it truly to help people."

Another colleague and captain II at LAFD, Erik Scott, said he could go on and on about how amazing Godinez is.

"Capt. Godinez is truly as good as they come," Scott said via email. "He is extremely well-versed in multiple areas on the fire ground and played a key role in many historic emergency incidents."

Scott added that Godinez's calm and competent disposition was not only ideal for handling stressful, emergency incidents, but also drew people to him.

"I loved working with him, and our members are very pleased that he is deservingly being awarded Firefighter of the Year," he said.

As Godinez's retirement and the award ceremony both fall in April, he believes there's no better way to end his career.

"I look at the past recipients that have won this, and they're legends on the job," Godinez said. "You hear their name, and if you're lucky, you've worked with them. … And, to now be in this same fraternity with them is just humbling to me, because I've never put myself in that category with them."

12

Social Media Has Unexpected Effects on Law Enforcement

Gwendolyn Waters

Captain Gwendolyn Waters is a police officer who has served with the San Bernardino Police Department in San Bernadino, California.

In the following viewpoint, Captain Gwendolyn Waters details the current risks to the safety of the lives of police officers in the United States. Waters showcases how, with the increased prevalence of the internet—including the fairly recent rise of social media—police officers face a challenge in their abilities to shield themselves from the repercussions of their jobs defending the community. Additionally, Waters details how police departments are navigating First Amendment rights as they work to protect their employees. One of the potential attacks Waters showcases is the ability for law enforcement officers to have their credibility attacked and how erroneous information can have the potential to reach a significant audience, including prospective jurors and internal affairs investigators.

Law enforcement always has been a dangerous profession because officers risk their lives to form a barrier between criminals and society. In the past, police could to some extent protect themselves and their loved ones from threats. Today these risks have changed. The power of the Internet—social media in

"Social Media and Law Enforcement," by Gwendolyn Waters, FBI Law Enforcement Bulletin, November 1, 2012.

particular—has brought danger home to officers and their families. They cannot shield themselves as easily from the repercussions of their jobs defending the community.

The Internet has been available for widespread public use since the early 1990s.[1] In its two decades of existence, the web has become an integral part of everyday life. It is difficult to recall how society functioned without it. Compared with the lifespan of the Internet, social media, which began to evolve in 2003, remains in its infancy. Users add their own content to any social media site that allows it.[2] Webpages, such as Facebook and Wikipedia, are not static; individuals continually modify them by adding commentary, photos, and videos. The web no longer is a fixed object for passive observation. It has become a dynamic venue for proactive—often passionate—interaction. The growth, power, and influence of social media have proven phenomenal as evidenced by the decline of traditional newspapers and the outcome of the 2008 presidential election.[3]

Law enforcement agencies recognize the influence of social media. Many departments are drafting and adopting policies addressing the use of networking engines.[4] In many cases, however, these plans miss a crucial part of the issue. While departments are concerned with minimizing the negative impact that speech not protected by the First Amendment may have on the department's interests, they sometimes may neglect their responsibility to protect their employees.

Characteristics

Information obtained from public records (e.g., birth, death, and real estate) has been available online for years. By increasing exposure of personal information, social media has raised the threat level. This new entity has a unique nature that makes it powerful and unpredictable. Several characteristics combine to make it especially threatening to law enforcement.

The structure of social media encourages self-promotion.[5] It offers easy access to an unlimited pool of potential "friends."[6] Individuals who crave validation can achieve a feeling of connection not available in their offline lives. People who have a desire for attention, notoriety, or fame are attracted to it. To get noticed, they often post entertaining or provocative information.

Constraints do not exist for social media. Anyone can post anything online with little fear of repercussion. The anonymous online environment can encourage inflammatory and shocking behavior. Individuals sometimes create screen names or new identities that allow them to act outside their normal inhibitions and sometimes participate in caustic and less ethical activities they otherwise would avoid. Anonymity hampers efforts to control these actions.[7]

Pooling of like minds often occurs online. This bolsters confidence and gives the impression of support for socially unacceptable conduct. Copycat behavior can make the first well-publicized transgression the impetus for many more. Social media can engender a mob mentality wherein one small stimulus spurs a wide-scale reaction that feeds on itself and grows out of control.[8] Incidents develop faster, reach farther, and spread more rapidly than anything society has dealt with before.

In the past, simple things, such as post office boxes and license plate confidentiality, provided protections. These are ineffective today. Instant access to private information makes it easier for an individual to learn personal facts about an officer. This also eliminates any "cooling off" period during which individuals might reconsider their retaliatory actions. Outraged offenders easily could get to officers' doorsteps before their patrol shifts end, leaving them unable to defend their homes or families. The combination of these factors—narcissism, anonymity, lack of restraint, copycat behavior, crowd mentality, and lack of a cooling off period—makes social media a uniquely significant force that constantly seeks a point of focus.

Focal Point

Characteristics intrinsic to law enforcement make it a natural focal point for this trend. In this public profession, officers' duties occur in a societal arena allotting them no privacy. Social media significantly has increased officers' community exposure. Police often are surrounded by cameras and amateur reporters who broadcast every action and their opinion of it to a worldwide audience. Due to its public nature, policing is an easy topic for network discussion.

To the community, law enforcement can be fascinating and contentious. It involves drama, intrigue, and excitement that society finds captivating. The number of crime dramas on television and in theaters validates this. Additionally, the police officer's role often is ambiguous to the public. Wrongdoers do not appreciate officers and may resent them. Police can represent controversial figures to some people.

Conflict with criminals is inherent to law enforcement. On a regular basis, police officers face lawless individuals. With increased exposure of personal information through social media, preventing these antagonists from crossing the line that separates officers' professional and personal lives is difficult. Prevention relies on self-restraint or respect for the law, neither of which are strengths of criminals.

Impact

The nature of social media and law enforcement makes their relationship particularly volatile. Few significant issues have been noted; however, the potential exists for police to be impacted by attacks on their credibility or through "cop baiting."[9]

Personal credibility is essential for law enforcement. Through social media, people easily can attack a police officer's character. If an officer's integrity is compromised, courtroom testimony and investigations are at risk. Law enforcement officers can find their honor under serious attack online at any time. Even erroneous information can reach a significant audience, to include potential jurors and internal affairs investigators, possibly causing irreparable damage to officers' reputations.

Cases have occurred where comments posted online by officers have led to disciplinary actions. These behaviors have been the key focus of social media policies currently in place. Postings by the public—over which departments have no control—can be more damaging. Regardless of their level of truth, negative comments create lasting impressions.

Empowered by social media, cop baiting presents a crisis for law enforcement. Questionable videos of police officers are popular on sites, such as YouTube, and can be financially rewarding to malefactors who file claims or lawsuits. For some individuals, a citation or jail time is worthwhile if a cash payoff results. Cop baiting could become so common that officers may not know whether they are facing a situation that is legitimate, staged, or exaggerated for someone else's benefit. This puts officers' personal and professional well-being at stake.

Threat

Considerable problems can occur, with the greatest danger being the personal threat to officers and their families. Because of social media, law enforcement officers are public figures more so than ever before. Barriers between their professional and personal lives have been diminished. Police may have no expectations that their homes and families will be protected from the dangers they face on the job.

Motivated individuals could destroy a law enforcement officer's sense of security without breaking any laws. With cell phone Internet access and a police officer's name, an antagonistic traffic violator could have a satellite image of the officer's home displayed on the phone by the time the officer returns to issue the citation. While this is not a violation of law, it certainly would send an intimidating message to the officer. A note could be left on the front door, or a photo of a child could be posted on a social networking site with a seemingly innocuous comment, such as, "Isn't officer so-and-so's daughter cute?"

Management

To protect their people, agencies can implement internal management mechanisms to lessen this potential threat. To provide the most effective protection, departments should designate a social media manager to handle specific core functions.

Ongoing training on current issues, the hazards of social media, and self-protection is essential. Due to the web's rapidly changing environment, one-time training is not sufficient. Individuals alone cannot keep up with social networking's constant evolution. A dedicated manager must ensure personnel are updated through e-mails, memoranda, briefings, and trainings.

The social media manager must facilitate the elimination of employees' personal data from social networking sites and guarantee consistency for all personnel. Most of these websites will remove information if petitioned to do so. Each has its own procedures for making that request. These sites must be monitored to ensure the files do not reappear.

Internet and social media alerts provide e-mail notification any time a specified word is mentioned or searched online. Many search engines offer these services free of charge. Personnel alerts could be directed to private e-mail accounts to avoid conflict with employee unions over privacy of off-duty activities. The social media manager would monitor agency alerts.

Many businesses have realized that paying attention to social media conversations can provide a wealth of information on consumer trends and product strengths and weaknesses. Law enforcement agencies could benefit from listening for commentary about the department and its programs and personnel. This would allow them to capitalize on their strengths and to identify and mitigate negative images or potential dangers. Providing the most effective protection against an impending attack requires identifying the risk early and strategizing a defense. Consistent monitoring of networking sites would provide an early warning system against any threats being developed or discussed online.

Monitoring trends and incidents that might precipitate copycat behavior is crucial. Attention must be paid to these activities because one quickly could precipitate others. Social media issues develop rapidly and spread extensively. The best defense against a threat is to recognize it early and identify ways to bolster the agency's defenses against it.

Agencies serve their best interests by protecting officers from dangers easily propagated through social media. Departments are impacted by claims or lawsuits, compromised officer credibility, damaged department image, and relocation expenses associated with plausible personal threats. Social networks present risks that law enforcement agencies must acknowledge. Hoping that large-scale impacts will not occur does not lessen the costs when they do; proactively addressing the possibility will.

Departments should initiate programs to foster awareness, education, and diligent management of employees' online exposure. These actions may not protect officers and agencies from the hazards social media presents, but they will minimize exposure and provide the greatest level of defense currently available.

Conclusion

It can be more cost effective to develop solutions after problems occur, rather than taking preventive actions that might not prove necessary. The concern with this approach is that the relationship between the police and social media is volatile. Social networks generate momentum, and law enforcement agencies provide a stimulus for that energy. Departments must take responsibility for protection from this threat before they become blindsided by a sudden viral attack on their officers.

Endnotes

1. Barry M. Leiner, Vinton G. Cerf, David D. Clark, Robert E. Kahn, Leonard Kleinrock, Daniel C. Lynch, Jon Postel, Larry G. Roberts, and Stephen Wolff, "Brief History of the Internet," Internet Society, December 2003, http://www.isoc.org/internet/history/brief.shtml (accessed September 10, 2012).
2. Andreas M. Kaplan and Michael Haenlein, "Users of the World, Unite! The Challenges and Opportunities of Social Media," *Business Horizons* 53, no. 1 (2010): 59-68.
3. Kaplan and Haenlein, 59–68; and "State of the News Media 2010 Executive Summary," The Pew Research Center's Project for Excellence in Journalism, http://www.stateofthemedia.org/2010/ chapter%20pdfs/2010_execsummary.pdf (accessed September 10, 2012); Jon Katz, "Online or Not, Newspapers Suck," *Wired* Magazine 2.09 (1994), http://www.wired.com/wired/archive/ 2.09news.suck.html (accessed September 10, 2012); Erik Qualman, *Socialnomics: How Social Media Transforms the Way We Live and Do Business* (New Jersey: John Wiley and Sons, 2009); and Michael Cornfield, "Yes, It Did Make a Difference," Taking Note, (2008), http://takingnote.tcf.org/2008/06/yes-it-did-make.html (accessed September 10, 2012).
4. Information and assistance on policy development can be found on the International Association of Chiefs of Police (IACP) Center for Social Media website at http://www.IACPsocialmedia.org/gettingstarted/policydevelopment (accessed September 10, 2012).
5. Christine Rosen, "Virtual Friendship and the New Narcissism," *The New Atlantis* no. 17 (Summer 2007): 15–31.
6. "Friends" on social networking sites include contacts whose profiles persons link to in their own profiles. On some sites, people have to accept the link; in others, they do not.
7. Deborah G. Johnson, "Ethics Online," Communications of the ACM 40, no. 1 (January 1997): 60–65; and Julie Zhuo, "Where Anonymity Breeds Contempt," *The New York Times*, November 29, 2010, http://www.nytimes.com/2010/11/30/opinion/30zhuo.html (accessed September 10, 2012).
8. Christian Russ, "Online Crowds—Extraordinary Mass Behavior on the Internet," http://i-know.tugraz.at/wp-content/uploads/2008/11/8_online-crowds.pdf (accessed September 10, 2012).
9. Cop baiting is when individuals intentionally create confrontational situations with officers to exploit them for personal or political motives.

13

Building Trust Between Police and the Communities They Serve Is Essential

John A. "Jack" Calhoun

Jack Calhoun has spent his entire career working to improve both the lives of those who live on society's edges and fragile families and neighborhoods from which they come. Calhoun helped found and direct Justice Resource Institute (JRI), an organization that pioneered Massachusetts's pre-trial diversion and restorative justice initiatives. JRI wrote and saw through to passage the nation's first pre-trial diversion law. As Massachusetts's commissioner of the Department of Youth Service, where he chaired the Adolescent and State of the Family Task Forces, he helped to create a comprehensive, community-based juvenile justice system that cut the state's recidivism rate to an astonishingly low10 percent.

Writing for the National League of Cities, Jack Calhoun discusses the efforts being taken to reckon with the historical role policing has taken in the creation of the racial inequities faced in current times. The author showcases the changes needed, emphasizing equality, transparency, accountability, shared information, and how police are trained, evaluated, and promoted. The viewpoint features quotes from people in a number of organizations, including the president of the International Association of Chiefs of Police and the president of the Police Foundation. It also points out the lack of research done on the effectiveness of the different efforts made to build police-community trust.

"Building Trust Between Police and the Communities They Serve," by John A. "Jack" Calhoun, National League of Cities, November 20, 2016. Reprinted by permission.

Municipal leaders can choose what kind of policing they will seek to provide to their constituents. In recent years, more have been choosing to place greater emphasis on police-community partnerships and the co-production of safety, which necessitates a strong focus on equity, transparency, accountability, shared information, and changes in how police are trained, evaluated and promoted.

> *There have been times when law enforcement officers, because of the laws enacted by federal, state, and local governments, have been the face of oppression for far too many of our fellow citizens. In the past, the laws adopted by our society have required police officers to perform many unpalatable tasks, such as ensuring legalized discrimination or even denying the basic rights of citizenship to many of our fellow Americans. While this is no longer the case, this dark side of our shared history has created a multigenerational—almost inherited—mistrust between many communities of color and their law enforcement agencies. Many officers who do not share this common heritage often struggle to comprehend the reasons behind this historic mistrust. As a result, they are often unable to bridge this gap and connect with some segments of their communities… The first step in this process is for law enforcement and the IACP to acknowledge and apologize for the actions of the past and the role that our profession has played in society's historical mistreatment of communities of color.—Terrence M. Cunningham, President, The International Association of Chiefs of Police*

In the wake of recent and highly-publicized shootings of both residents of color and police officers, many mayors and other city leaders are wrestling with these choices. In some communities, the resulting changes are sweeping and dramatic. For example, in the Watts section of Los Angeles, a neighborhood with mostly Black and Latino residents, new policies include a five-year residency requirement for sworn officers, co-screening of police by community members, and evaluation and promotion criteria based in large part on the quality and frequency of their community contacts and crime reduction in the neighborhoods they serve.

In cities like New Orleans and Tacoma, Washington, community conversations with law enforcement and residents of color are providing space for racial healing by acknowledging the historical role of policing in the creation of racial inequities. In other cities, elected officials are taking more incremental but still hopeful steps to strengthen ties between police and the community.

> *Enforcement is not the core of our work. Harm reduction, sustaining healthy communities and work with youth lie at our heart. We must co-produce safety with the community…we need training on the rightful role of police and training for mayors on hiring police chiefs, as public safety is their most important job and the chief of police is their most important hire.—Jim Bueermann, President, The Police Foundation*

Too little research has been done on the effectiveness of these efforts to know with certainty the most effective ways to build police-community trust. Nonetheless, a wealth of ideas and city examples give municipal officials many ways to get started. Five areas seem particularly promising for local action: engaging the community in planning and oversight; improving police training; promoting youth development; connecting residents to resources; and building personal relationships between police officers and residents. Here are a number of examples from each area:

Engaging the Community in Planning and Oversight

- Community conversations about race and police-community relations (many cities)
- Police and community working together to develop comprehensive violence prevention plans (many cities)
- MOUs that enhance data sharing and prevention planning
- "Micro-Community Policing Plans" (neighborhood safety plans developed with local residents in Seattle)
- Citizen Police Academies (many cities)
- "Community of Trust Committee" (Fairfax County, Virginia)
- Police/Clergy Advisory Boards (many cities)

- Police meeting with faith community following officer-involved shooting (Long Beach, California)
- Establishing success indicators to measure the progress of strategies to increase trust between law enforcement and the community
- Sharing plans with trusted community partners (e.g., local chapters of the NAACP and National Council of La Raza, the faith community)

Improving Training and Support for Police Officers

- Implicit bias training
- De-escalation of force training
- Cultural competency training
- Changing how officers are evaluated and promoted (Watts, California; Camden, New Jersey)
- Community service in Police Academy training (e.g., mentoring youth throughout academy training)
- "Transparency" policies
- Training police officers to police one another (New Orleans)
- Recruitment and hiring of minority and bilingual, bi-cultural law enforcement officers
- "Adopt a Cop" (e.g., churches praying for, caring for individual officers in San Jose, California)

Promoting and Supporting Youth Development

- Mentoring ("Youth Pride" in Providence; "Ambassadors Program" in Saint Paul)
- Tutoring (Santa Rosa, California; "OK" program in Oakland, California; PACER in Camden)
- Coaching football/basketball; police-athletic leagues (PAL in many cities)
- Chief's Youth Advisory Board (Louisville, Kentucky)
- Police Cadet Program (Los Angeles)
- Police Academy (Washington, D.C.)

- Explorer Scouts (many cities)
- "Challenges and Choices" taught by police in public schools (Los Angeles)
- "Officer Friendly" programs in schools
- Safety camps for youth (New Orleans)
- Youth/police dialogues (New Orleans, Seattle)
- Youth and Police Initiatives (Spokane; several sites in Massachusetts via Northeast Family Institute)

Connecting Residents to Community Resources

- Mental health clinicians riding with officers (Oakland); mental health officers (Madison, Wisconsin)
- Making citizens aware of essential services (e.g., homeless shelters, addiction treatment, housing and code enforcement)
- Social workers stationed in police departments (Boston)
- "Quality of Life Officers" (New Orleans)
- Community Policing Officers spotting and responding to non-enforcement problems such as poor lighting, absence of stop signs, local parks in disarray, problem bars (many cities)
- Diversion from arrest (Law Enforcement Assisted Diversion in many cities)
- Police/Human Services/School partnership to divert low-level offenders to services, which include school retention strategies (Philadelphia)
- Citation and release (Charleston, South Carolina)
- Officers linking caregivers to child protection agencies following arrest of a parent
- Police Departments supporting "Peacemaker or Street Worker" (Cure Violence) initiatives, most of which are staffed by ex-offenders

Building Personal Relationships Between Officers and Residents

- Pop Up Barbeques (Camden)
- Bike Patrols (Minneapolis, Minnesota; Covina, California)
- Operation Hoodsie (ice cream) Cup (Boston)
- Police/Youth Chats (Louisville)
- Coffee with a Cop, Coke with a Cop, Shop with a Cop (several cities)
- "Open Up" (police delivering food to people experiencing poverty in Knoxville, Tennessee)
- Police attending community meetings (many cities)
- Police worshipping in local churches/singing in choirs, attending local sport events & funerals
- Peace Walks with community groups (Long Beach; Boston; Richmond, California; Seattle)
- Help giving away food; planting trees (New Orleans)
- "Trust Talks" (Winston-Salem, North Carolina)
- Clergy (Baltimore) and citizen "Ride-Alongs" (many cities)
- Acknowledge need for reconciliation and for vehicles that promote trust
- Use of communication vehicles to share police programs, policies, practice

More Resources

- National League of Cities ("Policing in the 21st Century")
- President's Task Force on 21st Century Policing (recommendations derived from national hearings)
- The Police Foundation (evidence-based approaches to improve policing)

- The Police Executive Research Forum (program and policy research, TA provider, author of "Guiding Principles on Use of Force")
- International Association of Chiefs of Police (providing research, education on exemplary practice to its worldwide association of police professionals)
- S. Conference of Mayors ("Strengthening Police-Community Relations in America," a report by a working group of mayors and police chiefs)
- National Conference of State Legislators (policy actions states can take)
- National Alliance on Mental Illness (policing and the mentally ill)
- Campaign Zero (10 recommendations to reduce police violence from the community perspective)
- Vera Institute of Justice ("How to Support Trust Building in Your Agency") John Jay College, National Institute for Building Trust (initiative in six cities: Birmingham, Alabama; Fort Wayne, Indiana; Gary, Indiana; Minneapolis; Pittsburgh; Stockton, California)
- National Association of Counties (reports on various criminal justice issues)

14

US Cops Are Facing a Recruitment Crisis

J. D. Tuccille

J. D. Tuccille is a former managing editor of Reason.com and current contributing editor. Having started his online career in the days of proprietary online services and seen them swept away by the internet, he's a believer in the liberating and transformative power of new media.

In the following viewpoint, J. D. Tuccille details the recruiting challenges faced by numerous law enforcement agencies, including both the police and the FBI. In Montgomery County, Maryland, the number of people applying to be cops has dropped by half. The Bureau of Justice Statistics reports a decrease in police officers in the United States, including a drop of over 20,000 officers from 2013 to 2016. Tuccille asserts that this decrease may not be considered a negative thing, as the country considers other ways to keep the peace. He also points out the racial gap in perceptions of police officers, specifically the perceptions of African Americans.

The number of people applying to be cops in Montgomery County, Maryland, has dropped by half in recent years, according to a department complaint last week. Officials suggest it's because of growing national skepticism toward policing.

"US Cops Are Facing a Recruitment Crisis. Will It Force Them to Change Their Ways?" by J. D. Tuccille, Reason.com and *Reason* magazine, June 25, 2019. Reprinted by permission.

"When you do a job that's being highly criticized on a daily basis, we have to ask ourselves, how do we find good candidates that really want to be under that type of scrutiny," said Acting Police Chief Marcus Jones.

Montgomery County won't have an easy time importing its officers from other communities, either. Recruitment of law enforcement officers is down in areas around the country, and the drop in numbers is stark.

"The number of full-time sworn officers per 1,000 residents decreased, from 2.42 in 1997 to 2.17 in 2016," the Bureau of Justice Statistics (BJS) reported last summer. The raw number of police officers in the US also declined slightly, from 724,690 in 2013 to 701,169 in 2016.

Next door to Maryland, police departments in Virginia also saw declines in applications. So have departments in Minnesota, in Nashville, and in New York City, to name a few.

Nationally, 66 percent of police departments report seeing declining numbers of applications, according to a survey of 400 law enforcement agencies by the the Police Executive Research Forum (PERF).

The FBI suffers similar recruiting challenges, with special agent applicants plummeting from 68,500 in 2009 to 11,500 last year. This year, the Bureau doubled its recruitment advertising budget in an effort to attract more warm bodies.

These drops aren't necessarily a bad thing. The cop hiring crisis offers an opportunity for rethinking how we keep the peace in this country.

That opportunity could be squandered, however, if authorities don't address the problems of brutality and bias in police forces while resisting intrusive tactics that could make policing even nastier.

"The American policing profession may be facing the most fundamental questioning of its legitimacy in decades," said Chuck Wexler, executive director of the Police Executive Research Forum, in a 2017 organizational newsletter. "The very essence of policing is being debated in many cities, often because of controversial video recordings of police officers' actions. Community trust has eroded, and the professionalism of the police is being questioned."

A healthy job market gets some of the credit for the police recruitment crunch but, as Jones and Wexler describe, law enforcement has lost its gloss in the eyes of many Americans. Public opinion of law enforcement slid to a 22-year low in 2015, according to a Gallup poll.

Numbers have somewhat rebounded since, but that only emphasizes a racial gap in perceptions of police. African-Americans, in particular, tend to view cops as the government's enforcers rather than as protectors, amidst widely publicized racist incidents and concerns that their communities are disproportionately (and corruptly) targeted. In addition, a militarized police culture that arms officers with weapons of war and trains officers to treat the public as enemies worries those who feel targeted not over race, but just for not being cops.

The FBI has its own issues with declining support—especially among Republicans—after once again getting drawn into political shenanigans. Given the Bureau's history of misconduct, it's arguably to Americans' discredit that it took so long for us to become disenchanted.

Heavy-handed modern policing hasn't just alienated the public; it's decimated the pool of potential recruits.

"Some potential hires are ineligible to be considered because of prior arrests and convictions on minor criminal charges, such as possessing an open container of alcohol in public," PERF's Wexler points out. "This situation is especially prevalent in agencies that have practiced strict 'zero tolerance' policing in the past."

That last point may offer a key to improving relations between the public and what used to be known as "peace officers," by pursuing a less confrontational approach to policing.

"This militarized transformation of American law enforcement—and all that comes with it…should not be a part of the American landscape," former Los Angeles Police Department

Deputy Chief of Police Stephen Downing wrote for *Reason* five years ago. He went on to propose a program including ending drug prohibition, doing away with federal provision of military equipment and training to police departments, dumping civil asset forfeiture and its incentives to official banditry, reining-in search procedures, and establishing effective civilian oversight.

"With these kinds of reforms in place we could begin to heal our communities; diminish the mass incarceration of people of color; allow more parents to be with their children and fewer children to be sent to foster homes; recognize that addiction is a health rather than a criminal-justice problem, and supplant prison with treatment; abate the arms race between the police, gangs, and cartels; end police profiling; and restore the requirement of reasonable suspicion as an irrevocable feature of constitutional policing," he added.

Downing's proposals parallel, in many ways, the 2015 recommendations of the President's Task Force on 21st Century Policing. While stopping short of a retreat on drug prohibition, the task force's report noted, "law enforcement cannot build community trust if it is seen as an occupying force coming in from outside to impose control on the community." The report called for less-brutal tactics, consent-based searches, demilitarized police forces, and civilian oversight, among other changes.

The proposals were largely ignored at the time and pushed aside by the Trump administration's renewed emphasis on law-and-order policing even as crime rates continue their three-decade decline. But reformist ideas about restrained, less-intrusive policing aren't just philosophically attractive to those of us who care about liberty—they may help thinning police ranks reconcile with a hostile population.

Unfortunately, improvement isn't inevitable. Bad ideas abound, too.

"Contemporary researchers and police believe that they can… predict a crime before it happens—using computer algorithms," *Reason*'s Ron Bailey warned in 2016.

Police in some communities already adjust how they interact with people they meet based on risk scores assigned by computer algorithms. Cops like predictive policing because it lets them target anticipated trouble spots. But such tactics can become self-fulfilling.

"This creates a vicious cycle where police are sent to certain locations because the program predicts these locations to have the most crime, and the police begin to believe these same locations have the most crime because these were the locations to which they were sent," cautions the Electronic Frontier Foundation.

Dozens of cities have already deployed predictive policing software, *Vice* reported earlier this year. That means there's a good chance police will soon have a risk assessment appended to your name that will affect how much violence they bring to traffic stops and appearances at your door.

So, which will it be? Will law enforcement agencies rein-in their excesses and start interacting with the people around them as humans to be protected rather than as enemies to be dominated? Or will they instead assess us as committers of crimes that have yet to occur?

With their ranks diminishing and morale in the pits, policing will certainly change—for better or worse.

15

Law Enforcement Is Failing to Police Itself

Maddy Crowell and Sylvia Varnham O'Regan

Maddy Crowell is a freelance magazine journalist based in New York. She has filed stories from areas around the world, including South Asia, Europe, and Africa. Sylvia Varnham O'Regan is a New Zealand journalist who lives in New York and specializes in investigative reporting. Her work has appeared in the New York Times, GQ, *the* Atlantic, Guardian, Los Angeles Times, *and more.*

In the following viewpoint, Maddy Crowell and Sylvia Varnham O'Regan report on how, for decades, anti-government and white supremacist groups have been attempting to recruit police officers into their ranks. The authors share the story of a police officer in rural Alabama who was open about his affiliation with the League of the South, a group that believes white culture is threatened by forces including religious pluralism, homosexuality, and interracial coupling. The officer was promoted twice within the police department and even spoke at the group's annual conference. It was not until video of his speech leaked that he was dismissed from the department. This officer represents one of more than 100 scandals since 1990 in which police officers have made racist comments through emails, texts, and social media.

"Extremist Cops: How US Law Enforcement Is Failing to Police Itself," by Maddy Crowell and Sylvia Varnham O'Regan, Guardian News & Media Limited, December 13, 2019. Reprinted by permission.

Ever since he was a teenager, Joshua Doggrell has believed that the former slave-holding states of the American south should secede from the United States. When he was a freshman in college at the University of Alabama in 1995, Doggrell discovered a group whose worldview chimed with his—the League of the South. The League believes that white southern culture is in danger of extinction from forces such as religious pluralism, homosexuality and interracial coupling. Doggrell wanted to protect that culture. In 2006, when he was 29 years old, he applied to be a police officer in Anniston, Alabama, a sparsely populated city at the foothills of the Appalachian mountains, where more than half of the residents are people of colour. On his police application, Doggrell wrote that he was a member of the League. Shortly after, he was hired.

During nearly a decade on the police force, Doggrell was a vocal advocate for the League, working to recruit fellow officers to the group. He encouraged his colleagues to attend the League's monthly meetings, which he held at a steakhouse not far from the police station. On Facebook, he posted neo-Confederate material, including a photo of an early leader of the Ku Klux Klan, and wrote that he was "against egalitarianism in all forms." He often refused to be in the room when the department recited the pledge of allegiance in front of the American flag.

In 2013, Doggrell delivered the opening speech at the League's annual conference, on how to "cultivate the good will" of police officers. "The vast majority of men in uniform are aware that they're southerners," Doggrell told the audience, which included the prominent neo-Nazi Matthew Heimbach and another Anniston police officer Doggrell had recruited to the group. Doggrell added that most southern officers were "a lot closer" to joining the League than they were 10 or 15 years ago. "My department," he added, "has been very supportive of me. I've somehow been promoted twice since I was there."

"Everybody knew he was in the League of the South," Matt Delozier, a retired sergeant from the Anniston police department, told us when we met him near Anniston earlier this year. "I think the general consensus was that nobody understood—if you're out here in law enforcement in a supervisor's role, why are you involved in this group?" But it wasn't until 2015, when a leaked video of Doggrell's speech led to a report that went viral across the US, that the city's manager fired him. (Doggrell's superiors did not raise any concerns over his conduct as an officer.) Doggrell went on to appeal the dismissal and sue both the city and the city manager, arguing that his termination had violated his constitutional rights.

Although it is unusual for a police officer to be so open about his involvement in an extremist organisation, for decades, anti-government and white-supremacist groups have been attempting to recruit police officers into their ranks. "It is something a lot of folks are overlooking," says Vida B. Johnson, an assistant professor of law at Georgetown University. "Police forces are becoming more interested in talking about implicit bias—the unconscious, racial biases we carry with us as Americans. But people aren't really addressing the explicit biases that are present on police forces."

According to Johnson's research, there have been at least 100 different scandals, in more than 40 different states, involving police officers who have sent racist emails and text messages, or made racist comments on social media, since the 1990s. A recent investigation by the Center for Investigative Reporting found that hundreds of active-duty and retired law enforcement officers from around the country were members of confederate, anti-government and anti-Islam groups on Facebook. But there is no official record of officers who are tied to white supremacist or other extremist groups because, in the US, there is no federal policy for screening or monitoring the country's 800,000+ law enforcement officers for extremist views. The 18,000 or so police departments across the country are largely left to police themselves.

To much of the rest of the country, the town of Anniston, Alabama, is primarily known as the site of a traumatic episode in the American civil rights movement. On 14 May 1961, the Freedom Riders, a group of black and white civil rights activists, arrived by bus in Anniston to protest segregation. They were attacked by a mob of Ku Klux Klansmen, who slashed the bus's tyres, broke its windows and set fire to it in an attempt to kill the protesters. Even though the Anniston police department was only a block away, the officers didn't show up on the scene until the early afternoon, and made no arrests.

Today, Anniston remains sharply divided along racial lines. The majority of the city's black community lives southwest of downtown, in run-down, single-storey houses. East of the city centre, manicured lawns and picket fences adorn the predominantly white neighbourhood. Although roughly 50% of the city's 24,000 residents are black, the people who govern the city are mostly white. "It always comes down to leadership," said David E. Reddick, one of the city's two black council members and a former president of the local chapter of the National Association for the Advancement of Colored People, when we met in his office. "You've got a city where you've got three whites and two blacks on the council, and you need three votes to get anything done."

"Blacks are being targeted in this city," Reddick continued. According to the city's other black council member, Ben Little, its officers regularly pull black people over for minor offences such as traffic violations. Little also said that members of the police department had often intimidated and harassed him, or stood by while others did. After being particularly vocal in his criticisms of police abuses in 2012, he woke up one morning to find caution tape wrapped like a noose around his truck. When Little and Reddick voiced their concerns about local policing two years ago, the local newspaper, the *Anniston Star*, responded with the headline: "NAACP leaders, with little evidence, claim racism by police, courts."

Joshua Doggrell claims that his views are not unusual in Anniston. "My people are Southern people and we grew up proud of our Southern heritage," he told us, when we met him at a restaurant where he used to host League of the South meetings. He is solidly built, with a round, puffy face, and drove a black pickup truck with Confederate flags on the front bumper. He insisted that he was not a racist or a white supremacist, and claims that he had ceased his involvement with the League by early 2015, but admitted he thought "there are some things the white race did better throughout the history of mankind, like governing." He couched his extremist views in careful terms, often centred on his religious beliefs: he wasn't "against blacks," he claimed—he just didn't believe God had created the races to be mixed.

Doggrell presented himself as a victim who had been wronged by the city when he was fired from the police department. When he joined the force in 2006, none of his superiors flagged his membership in the League of the South as an issue, he told us. (The police department refused multiple requests for interviews.) Three years later, Doggrell started a local chapter of the League, and invited a number of fellow officers to its first meeting. At the meeting, the League's founder, a former history professor named Michael Hill, argued that the time had come for a new civil war. "The way I look at it," Hill told the group, "this is round two of the same battle."

The department's tolerance for Doggrell seemed to be mirrored by some of the local press. When Doggrell held his League chapter's first meeting, in an Anniston diner, he invited a reporter from the *Anniston Star* to cover it. The *Star* published a 380-word account of the meeting that read like the announcement of a new seniors' night at the bingo hall: "Local Secessionists Hold 1st Meeting."

But several people of colour in Anniston recognised Doggrell's name in the report and were alarmed. Abdul Khalil'llah, the director of an Anniston-based civil rights organisation, sent letters to the Alabama attorney general's office and the US secretary of homeland security in April 2009. "I was basically astonished to hear that a police officer—someone who'd taken an oath to uphold the law—could be in a neo-Confederate type of organisation," Khalil'llah said.

Khalil'llah's letters went unanswered, but in response to his complaints, the Anniston police department decided to conduct an internal investigation into Doggrell later that year. A few officers had found Doggrell's views odd, but the department decided to take no action against him. "He is a dedicated, professional police officer," then police chief, John Dryden, wrote in a report. "He has never showed any radical action in his duties as a police officer." It was not a concern to the police department that Doggrell was part of an organisation that the Southern Poverty Law Center, which monitors rightwing extremist organisations, had labelled a "hate group" since 2000. (The SPLC "can label anything," Dryden wrote in the report.)

Not long after the investigation, Doggrell was promoted to sergeant and then, a few years later, to lieutenant. Doggrell's former boss, Layton McGrady, acknowledged at a 2015 hearing into Doggrell's dismissal that Doggrell's association with the League of the South wasn't a factor when he was up for promotion. Asked why not, McGrady said it "didn't affect his job performance or the police department."

While not every police officer who is tied to a white supremacist group will necessarily act out their beliefs violently, the presence of even a single radicalised officer can terrorise a community. "Even if the number of officers is numerically small, because of the intense risks posed of having a ticking time bomb like that in a department, that's a big deal," said Brian Levin, a former NYPD officer who directs the Center for the Study of Hate and Extremism in California.

In a number of cases, ideologically radicalised police officers have gone on to commit extreme forms of violence. In one of the most disturbing cases, a civil rights lawsuit from 1991 alleged that a group of officers from the Los Angeles county sheriff's department systematically terrorised and harassed minority residents by vandalising their homes, beating and torturing them, and even killing members of the community. The accused officers turned out to be members of the Lynwood Vikings, a "neo-Nazi, white supremacist gang," according to a federal judge. (The county settled the case for $9m.) In 2012, an officer in Little Rock, Arkansas, who had once attended a KKK meeting, shot and killed a 15-year-old black boy. Earlier this year, in Holton, Michigan, an officer was fired after a framed KKK application and Confederate flags were discovered in his home.

"Since the inception of this nation, black people have been under threat from the police," said Whitney Shepard, who works at the DC-based organisation Stop Police Terror Project. "There's not really ever been a time in this country where the police have protected our communities."

In 2006, a leaked report from the FBI's counterterrorism division warned that white supremacists have spent decades trying to "infiltrate law enforcement communities or recruit law enforcement personnel." The document, first reported on by the *Intercept*, noted that the term "ghost skins" had gained currency among white supremacists, to describe extremists who "avoid overt displays of their beliefs to blend into society and covertly advance white supremacist causes."

But experts have difficulty gauging the number of white supremacists within law enforcement. Some give ballpark figures in the low hundreds, while others can't give an estimate at all. This has led some to downplay the issue. "Let's say you've got thousands that are sympathetic or members of extremist groups," a former FBI analyst said to us. "Is that a big deal? It's not good, obviously, because police officers do have such great power, but I wouldn't say it's a huge problem."

The problem may be growing, though. "We're seeing the radical right rise in substantial ways, and inevitably that is reflected in police forces and security forces more generally," said Mark Potok, a senior fellow at the Centre for Analysis of the Radical Right. Although the FBI keeps tabs on white supremacist and other types of extremist groups operating within the US, it typically only mounts full investigations when there's a reasonable indication of criminal activity. The Bureau may know of some officers who are active members of white supremacist organisations, but it maintains that it's not the FBI's place to remove them from police forces unless they violate federal law. "We do not and will not police ideology," an FBI spokesperson wrote in an email, after the Bureau denied repeated requests for an interview.

"It's astonishing to me that we have an FBI that acknowledges these white-supremacist police officers exist and they don't have any plan to address it," said Michael German, a former FBI agent and current fellow at the Brennan Center for Justice. "Or to protect the communities who they're obligated to protect under the civil rights laws."

In the speech that eventually got him fired, Doggrell spoke about the importance of recruiting police officers to the League of the South, and resisting the federal government's interference in their communities. "Kith and kin comes before illegal national mandates," he said.

When people in Anniston's black community found out about Doggrell's speech, "it was like another Ferguson in Anniston," David Reddick, the city council member, said, referring to the mass protests that had shaken Ferguson, Missouri, after a police officer there killed an unarmed black teenager named Michael Brown. "It had that feeling that it could break out at any moment."

Two days after the SPLC's report about Doggrell's speech went viral, Anniston's city manager fired him. (The other police officer who had joined the League, Wayne Brown, retired.) The department portrayed Doggrell's case as an aberration, even though it had tolerated his ideology for years. "This anomaly should not end up characterising that department at all," the mayor said. In response, Doggrell appealed his dismissal on the basis of wrongful termination, and filed a separate claim stating his free speech and religious rights had been violated. Both were denied; but his wrongful termination appeal is still pending with the circuit court of Calhoun County. The League of the South helped to raise between $10,000 and $15,000 to cover his legal fees.

The reason that extremist groups are allowed to exist in the US is because of the first amendment to the constitution, which ostensibly protects all citizens' freedom of expression. In many European countries, the law prohibits membership of hate groups that express explicitly racist, neo-Nazi, antisemitic or homophobic views. The question in the US is whether free speech rights apply to law enforcement officers and other public servants in the same way as they do to private citizens.

In Anniston, many people saw Doggrell's membership in the League as an extension of his rights. "There's first-amendment issues that have to be addressed if you are going to terminate someone for being a member of that group," said Bruce Downey, the attorney who defended the city against Doggrell's lawsuit, when we met at his office in July. That Doggrell was within his constitutional rights to be both in the police department and in the League seemed to be accepted inside the department, too. At the 2015 hearing into Doggrell's dismissal, Anniston's police chief acknowledged he had seen content he considered "edgy at best" on Doggrell's Facebook page, but he hadn't taken any action. "Social media is an issue with all of our officers, I will tell you that," he said. "We don't make it a habit of monitoring. As a matter of fact, we don't monitor."

To others, however, the US's full complement of free speech rights does not extend to law enforcement officers. "There are limitations on what government employees can do, especially where their speech implicates their ability to do their jobs properly," said Chiraag Bains, the former senior counsel to the head of the Justice Department's civil rights division. "So, if they're associating with a white supremacist group, it's within the police department's authority to say that the person cannot do that job." Bains added that police officers are sworn to uphold the constitution, which promises equal treatment under the law to all Americans, regardless of race. The US court of appeals, too, has found that the "interest in maintaining a relationship of trust between the police and fire departments and the communities they serve" outweighs officers' right to free expression.

Had the video of Doggrell's speech never gone viral, though, it's quite likely he would still be serving on the Anniston police force. Regardless of what the courts decide about officers' free speech rights, it's exceptionally difficult for private citizens to force local departments to take action against extremists within their ranks.

In the three years since President Trump has been in office, white supremacists have become increasingly emboldened. The deadly "Unite the Right" rally in 2017, in which 600 far-right supporters clashed with anti-racist protesters in Charlottesville, Virginia, was a "wake-up call" that white supremacist groups were resurgent, said the Anti-Defamation League. But despite the fact that white supremacists and far-right extremists have killed more people in the US in the last decade than adherents of any other ideology have, the Trump administration has done little to address the threat. Instead, it has reduced the federal oversight of white supremacist groups. Soon after taking office, Trump cut the Department of Homeland Security's budget for terrorism prevention, which includes domestic terrorism, from $24m in 2017 to $3m today, according to the former Obama administration counterterrorism official Nate Snyder.

In 2018, attorney general Jeff Sessions—a former Alabama senator who once joked that he thought KKK members "were OK until I learned they smoked pot"—signed a memorandum that restricted the Justice Department's ability to oversee troubled police departments, including the 14 that had agreed to be monitored under the Obama administration because of their records of racial discrimination and police abuse. "The misdeeds of individual bad actors," Sessions wrote, "should not impugn or undermine the legitimate and honorable work that law enforcement officers and agencies perform in keeping American communities safe."

Earlier this year, the FBI revealed that it had changed its classification system for terrorism cases. While there were once 11 categories, including a specific one for white supremacy, the new list featured just four, including the catch-all "racially motivated violent extremism." This change means it's now harder to narrow down exactly what resources the FBI is putting toward the specific threat of white supremacy, including within police forces.

Yet when it comes to policing police officers for extremist ties, the FBI has not changed its policy since the civil rights era, said German, the former FBI agent. "Many of these cases end up resting on kind of weak grounds where it's only if a person posts something on social media, or otherwise publicises their role in a way that damages the public perception of the police agency, that the agency can take action," he added. "I'm more concerned about the guy who's a white supremacist who is not making it public, and is perhaps engaged in behaviour on the job that is harming people on a daily basis."

Still, it's unclear whether greater federal oversight would actually solve the problem. "In theory it could help, but that means we would have to not have a broken democracy," said Shepard of the activist group Stop Police Terror Project. "We'd have to have folks that would take the accountability measure seriously and I honestly at this point do not have faith in that happening for black people." Mark Potok, from the Centre for Analysis of the Radical Right, made a similar point: "At this point, since the election of Trump, we've seen so many cases of strongly racist cops—it's become even more imperative to put these departments on some kind of oversight from outside. And really, I'm talking about civilian review boards."

In Anniston, things have mostly stayed the same since Doggrell was fired. After Doggrell's termination, according to Reddick, the police department began hiring more diverse staff. It also started requiring each of its officers to affirm in writing that he or she was "not a member of a group that will cause embarrassment to the City of Anniston or the Anniston police department." But the council's black leaders are still outnumbered, and the city is still divided. In July, a group of residents proposed redrawing the city limits to exclude Anniston's black neighbourhoods.

A number of residents we spoke to in Anniston remained unsure of why exactly Doggrell had been fired. "I heard he was an exemplary police officer, in a biracial relationship, and no signs of racism," one of the three white council members wrote in an email. (Doggrell is not in a biracial relationship and does not condone those who are.) Unprompted, during our interview, the lawyer Bruce Downey, who defended the city against Doggrell's lawsuit, said he thought Doggrell was a "very intelligent guy and a deep thinker."

To Anniston council member Ben Little, the city's black residents are still fighting a similar battle to the one his enslaved ancestors fought—one that was not exclusively against the police department, but against the "racial backwardness" of a city that treated its minority population with "oppression and inequality." Nobody in the community was surprised to find out that a member of the police force had belonged to a neo-Confederate group, he added. "They were only surprised that it was so bold and out there," he said. "But we knew it all along."

16

Why Are Ambush Killings of Police on the Rise?

Jared Keller

Jared Keller is deputy editor at Task & Purpose. *His writing has also appeared in* Aeon, Brooklyn Magazine, GQ, Lapham's Quarterly, *the* Los Angeles Review of Books, Outside, Slate, Smithsonian, *the* Verge, VICE, *the* Village Voice, *and many other publications.*

In the following viewpoint, Jared Keller details the 300 percent increase in police officers who were targeted in "ambush killings" in 2016. While the number of police officer killings has decreased over the last 40 years, there has been an uptick in recent years. The author goes on to account for the reasons behind the increase, including both the Black Lives Matter and Blue Lives Matter movements. Additionally, Keller discusses the rise of the "sovereign citizen" ideology, pointing out its racist origins, and how recent research from the University of Maryland's National Consortium for the Study of Terrorism and Responses to Terrorism has shown that "sovereign citizens" pose a greater domestic threat than Islamic terrorists.

"Why Are Ambush Killings of Police on the Rise?" by Jared Keller, The Social Justice Foundation, December 1, 2016. Reprinted by permission.

The week of Thanksgiving, a 19-year-old gunman was shot and killed after ambushing a police officer in St. Louis, Missouri. The 46-year-old sergeant, who miraculously survived the two bullets to the head, wasn't the only victim of an ambush-style attack that day: A San Antonio police officer was fatally shot during a traffic stop in what local police described as "a targeted killing similar to recent police shootings in Dallas and Baton Rouge, Louisiana," according to CNN. The cable news network reported that the San Antonio and St. Louis attacks were two of four such attacks that rankled police forces across the country—all on the same day.

What looks like an unnerving coincidence may signal a more disturbing trend. A recent mid-year report from the National Law Enforcement Officers Memorial Fund, which quantifies police officer deaths, showed that 67 federal, state, and local law enforcement officers were killed as of July 20th, 2016, up 8 percent over last year; more alarmingly, some 14 officers were fatally targeted in "ambush killings," a 300 percent increase from the three ambush killings that took place during the same time period in 2015. The recent ambushes, including those that took place on the Sunday before Thanksgiving, bring the total to 20. And those are just officers who died in the line of duty: The Federal Bureau of Investigation's crime statistics suggest that 240 police officers were ambushed in 2015.

While the NLEOMF's own data shows that police officer killings have declined sharply over the last 40 years alongside the national crime rate—including ambush assaults, which a *Washington Post* analysis shows have dropped significantly from 1990 to 2014—the sudden uptick in officer ambushes has made police forces increasingly nervous. In July, just before the release of the NLEOMF's mid-year report, Army veteran Micah Johnson gunned down five police officers during a protest against the mistreatment of African Americans by police in Dallas, Texas; just a few days latter, Gavin Long murdered three police officers in Baton Rouge. Despite a decline in violent crime, it now seems more and more dangerous to be a police officer in America.

But how do we account for this uptick in police ambushes? The go-to answer among some law enforcement officials is cut and dry: Blame the rhetoric of the Black Lives Matter movement for inciting a "War on Cops," as was the case in the aftermath of the Dallas and Baton Rogue ambushes this summer. In the aftermath of the Dallas attack, the National Association of Police Organizations blamed "senseless agitators and gutless politicians"—including the Department of Justice's Civil Rights Division—"who helped bring about these murders." Conservative pundits blamed "race hustlers" like Reverend Al Sharpton; the Manhattan Institute's Heather Mac Donald devoted a whole book to arguing that anti-police rhetoric "spawned riots, 'die-ins,' and the assassination of police officers" by African Americans. And, as recently as this November, the father of a slain Dallas police officer sued the leaders of the Black Lives Matter organization, a "violent and revolutionary criminal gang," for inciting "further violence, severe bodily injury and death against police officers of all races and ethnicities, Jews, and Caucasians."

Consider Harris County, Texas, Sheriff Ron Hickman's statement to the *Huffington Post* after one of his deputies was ambushed while pumping gas late last year:

> *The general climate of that kind of rhetoric can be influential on people to do things like this. We're still searching to find out if that's actually a motive, We've heard black lives matter, all lives matter. Well, cops' lives matter, too. So how about we drop the qualifier and just say lives matter?*

Despite the fact that leaders and activists associated with the Black Lives Matter movement were quick to condemn the ambush-style attacks on police in Dallas and Baton Rouge this summer, the relationship between civil rights activism and police ambushes has only gained traction since it metastasized nearly two years ago. In December of 2014—in the midst of nationwide protests against police mistreatment of African Americans following the non-indictment of New York Police Department officer Daniel Pantaleo in the choking death of Staten Island resident Eric Garner—NYPD officers Rafael Ramos and Wenjian Liu were gunned down in their squad car by Ismaaiyl Brinsley in "revenge" for the deaths of Garner and Michael Brown. The deaths of Ramos and Liu helped give birth to the "Blue Lives Matter" pro-police movement, which was aided and abetted by the law-and-order rhetoric that marked the 2016 presidential campaign trail.

But, anecdotally, it's not totally clear that there's a direction connection between the rise of anti-police rhetoric and these ambushes. Yes, the perpetrators of high-profile police ambushes like Brinsley in New York and Johnson in Dallas targeted police in response to racial disparities in the criminal justice system (according to Dallas police chief David Brown, Johnson "was upset about the recent police shootings … upset at white people," and "stated he wanted to kill white people, especially white officers," per the *New York Times*).

But Baton Rouge gunman Gavin Long, despite his rantings over the death of unarmed black men at the hands of police, appeared motivated more by the anti-government "sovereign citizen" movement and had a history of paranoia and delusion. And Scott Michael Greene, who killed two Des Moines police officers earlier this month in a highway ambush, was a middle-aged white man who had been previously arrested for waving a Confederate flag at a high school football game—hardly the Black Lives Matter sympathizer.

These examples point to a complicating factor that somewhat muddies arguments claiming the anti-police rhetoric of the current racial justice movement is entirely to blame for the recent "war on cops": the rise of the "sovereign citizen" ideology among Americans both white and black. In 2011, the FBI issued warnings to federal, state, and local law enforcement agents around the threats posed by sovereign citizens, the same year that a Southern Policy Law Center report observed a rise in the adoption of sovereign citizen philosophies and tactics by African-American radicals independent of the Black Lives Matter movement's governing philosophy, as was the case with Long:

> *"The movement of sovereign citizens—most of whom are clearly unaware of the ideology's racist roots—has grown extremely rapidly in the last two or three years," the SPLC said in a statement. "And, while black Americans remain a relatively small fraction of the estimated 300,000 sovereign citizens nationwide, it seems clear that their numbers are growing."*

While anti-police rhetoric may have heightened attention to post-Ferguson police ambushes, sovereign citizens have been responsible for a growing number of attacks on police in the last several years, including the 2014 shooting spree by heavily armed Jerad and Amanda Miller in Las Vegas. A 2014 study from the University of Maryland's National Consortium for the Study of Terrorism and Responses to Terrorism, released in the weeks between Garner and Brown's deaths that summer, found that law enforcement agencies overwhelmingly saw sovereign citizens as a greater domestic threat than even Islamic terrorists.

Even NLEOMF president Craig W. Floyd agrees that politicians and police advocates are overlooking the threat posed by anti-government vigilantes of all racial backgrounds. "So much dialogue has centered around race relations, but there is a hatred in this country right now that's just gotten out of control," he told Fox News after the Houston and Baton Rouge attacks last week. "There is a lack of respect for government in general, and the most visible and vulnerable symbol of government in America is patrolling our streets in marked cars." In the case of these police ambushes, it would seem motives are more complicated than mere racial identity.

This, of course, doesn't excuse the violent attacks of self-styled vigilantes who mow down police officers in the name of "justice," but it does suggest that the correlation between the post-Brown era of civil rights activism and the War on Cops is complicated at best. Unfortunately, there's a major obstacle to untangling the root causes of the War on Cops, and that's the way data on crime and violence in the United States is reported and analyzed. It's possible that the rise in police ambushes is a function of the overall 10.8 percent increase in homicides in the last year, an increase that, while significant, does not significantly untangle the specific geography (and, in turn, sociopolitical history) that determines a state or city's relationship with criminal violence.

It's also worth noting, per the *Post*'s Christopher Ingraham, that NLEOMF and the FBI's ambush and police shooting statistics "are subject to significant year-over-year fluctuation in part because these incidents are so rare." And all of these changes take place against the backdrop of both a historically low crime rate and a comparatively low rate of police deaths. While the existing crime data does not uniformly place the blame at the feet of civil rights activists fighting for justice and reform in their local police department, it does suggest that something is deeply wrong in the relationship between law enforcement agencies and the communities they're meant to police.

Organizations to Contact

The editors have compiled the following list of organizations concerned with the issues debated in this book. The descriptions are derived from materials provided by the organizations. All have publications or information available for interested readers. The list was compiled on the date of publication of the present volume; the information provided here may change. Be aware that many organizations take several weeks or longer to respond to inquiries, so allow as much time as possible.

American Civil Liberties Union
125 Broad Street, 18th Floor
New York, NY 10004
(212) 549-2500
email: info@aclu.org
website: www.aclu.org

The ACLU evolved from a small group of idealists into the nation's premier defender of the rights enshrined in the US Constitution. With more than 1.5 million members, nearly 300 staff attorneys, thousands of volunteer attorneys, and offices throughout the nation, the ACLU of today continues to fight government abuse and to vigorously defend individual freedoms, including speech and religion, a woman's right to choose, the right to due process, citizens' rights to privacy, and much more. The ACLU stands up for these rights even when the cause is unpopular, and sometimes when nobody else will. While we might not always agree on every issue, Americans have come to count on the ACLU for its unyielding dedication to principle. The ACLU has become so ingrained in American society that it is hard to imagine an America without it.

Black Lives Matter

email: available via contact form on website
website: www.blacklivesmatter.com

Black Lives Matter was founded in 2013 in response to the acquittal of Trayvon Martin's murderer. Black Lives Matter Global Network Foundation, Inc., is a global organization in the US, UK, and Canada, whose mission is to eradicate white supremacy and build local power to intervene in violence inflicted on Black communities by the state and vigilantes. By combating and countering acts of violence, creating space for Black imagination and innovation, and centering Black joy, the organization is winning immediate improvements in our lives.

The Cato Institute

1000 Massachusetts Ave NW
Washington, DC 20001
(202) 842-0200
email: info@cato.org
website: www.cato.org

The Cato Institute is a public policy research organization—a think tank—dedicated to the principles of individual liberty, limited government, free markets, and peace. Its scholars and analysts conduct independent, nonpartisan research on a wide range of policy issues. Founded in 1977, Cato owes its name to *Cato's Letters*, a series of essays published in 18th- century England that presented a vision of society free from excessive government power. Those essays inspired the architects of the American Revolution. And the simple, timeless principles of that revolution—individual liberty, limited government, and free markets—turn out to be even more powerful in today's world of global markets and unprecedented access to information than Jefferson or Madison could have imagined. Social and economic freedom is not just the best policy for a free people, it is the indispensable framework for the future.

Center for Policing Equity

1925 Century Park East #1700
Los Angeles, CA 90067
(347) 948-9953
email: comms@policingequity.org
website: www.policingequity.org

As a research and action think tank, the Center for Policing Equity (CPE) produces analyses identifying and reducing the causes of racial disparities in law enforcement. Using evidence-based approaches to social justice, it uses data to create levers for social, cultural, and policy change. The Center for Policing Equity also holds a 501(c)3 status. Using the power of science, CPE uses advanced analytics to diagnose disparities in policing, shed light on police behavior, and answer questions police and communities have asked for years about how to build a healthy relationship.

The Marshall Project

156 West 56th Street, Suite 701
New York, NY 10019
(212) 803-5200
email: info@themarshallproject.org
website: www.themarshallproject.org

The Marshall Project is a nonpartisan, nonprofit news organization that seeks to create and sustain a sense of national urgency about the US criminal justice system. It works to achieve this through award-winning journalism, partnerships with other news outlets, and public forums. The organization strives to educate and enlarge the audience of people who care about the state of criminal justice.

National Association of Police Organizations (NAPO)

317 South Patrick Street
Alexandria, VA 22314-3501
(703) 549-0775
email: info@napo.org
website: www.napo.org

The National Association of Police Organizations is a coalition of police unions and associations from across the United States and was organized for the purpose of advancing the interests of America's law enforcement officers through legislative advocacy, political action, and education. Increasingly, the rights and interests of law enforcement officers have been the subject of legislative, executive, and judicial action in the nation's capital. NAPO works to influence the course of national affairs where law enforcement interests are concerned.

National Consortium for the Study of Terrorism and Responses to Terrorism

PO Box 266
5245 Greenbelt Rd
College Park, MD 20740
(301) 405-6600
email: infostart@start.umd.edu
website: www.start.umd.edu

The National Consortium for the Study of Terrorism and Responses to Terrorism—better known as START—is a university-based research and education center comprised of an international network of scholars committed to the scientific study of the causes and human consequences of terrorism in the United States and around the world. A Department of Homeland Security Emeritus Center of Excellence headquartered at the University of Maryland, START supports the research efforts of leading social scientists at more than 50 academic and research institutions, each of whom is conducting original investigations into fundamental questions about terrorism.

National Initiative for Building Community Trust and Justice

John Jay College of Criminal Justice
524 West 59th Street, Suite 600
New York, NY 10019
(212) 393-6457
email: ahatch@jjay.cuny.edu
website: www.trustandjustice.org

The National Initiative for Building Community Trust and Justice is a project to improve relationships and increase trust between communities and the criminal justice system and advance the public and scholarly understandings of the issues contributing to those relationships. In September 2014, the US Department of Justice announced a three-year, $4.75 million grant to establish the project. In collaboration with the Department of Justice, the National Initiative is coordinated by the National Network for Safe Communities at John Jay College of Criminal Justice, with partnership from the Justice Collaboratory at Yale Law School, the Center for Policing Equity at John Jay College, and UCLA, and the Urban Institute.

National Institute of Justice

810 7th Street NW
Washington, DC 20531
(202) 307-0703
email: ojp.ocom@usdoj.gov
website: www.nij.ojp.gov

NIJ is the research, development, and evaluation agency of the US Department of Justice. It is dedicated to improving knowledge and understanding of crime and justice issues through science, and provides objective and independent knowledge and tools to inform the decision making of the criminal and juvenile justice communities to reduce crime and advance justice, particularly at the state and local levels.

National Law Enforcement Officers Memorial Fund

444 E Street NW
Washington DC, 20001
(202) 737-3405
email: info@nleomf.org
website: www.nleomf.org

The National Law Enforcement Officers Memorial Fund is dedicated to telling the story of American law enforcement and making it safer for those who serve. The Memorial Fund built and continues to maintain the National Law Enforcement Officers Memorial—the nation's monument to law enforcement officers killed in the line of duty. The Memorial Fund is a principal organizer of the National Police Week observance each May and hosts a candlelight vigil each May 13 to honor all fallen officers. In addition, the Memorial Fund maintains the largest, most comprehensive database of line-of-duty officer deaths, conducts research into officer fatality trends and issues, and serves as an information clearinghouse.

National Police Foundation

2550 S Clark Street, Suite 1130
Arlington, VA 22202
(202) 833-1460
email: info@policefoundation.org
website: www.policefoundation.org

The National Police Foundation's mission is to advance policing through innovation and science. It is the oldest nationally known, nonprofit, nonpartisan, and non-membership-driven organization dedicated to improving America's most noble profession—policing.

National Public Safety Partnership

email: available via contact form on website
website: www.nationalpublicsafetypartnership.org

The National Public Safety Partnership (PSP) was established in June 2017 by the US Department of Justice (DOJ) in response to President Trump's Executive Order on a Task Force on Crime Reduction and Public Safety, which emphasizes the role of DOJ in combating violent crime. It states: "The Department of Justice shall take the lead on federal actions to support law enforcement efforts nationwide and to collaborate with state, tribal, and local jurisdictions to restore public safety to all of our communities." PSP provides an innovative framework for DOJ to enhance its support of state, tribal, and local law enforcement officers and prosecutors in the investigation, prosecution, and deterrence of violent crime, especially crime related to gun violence, gangs, and drug trafficking. This approach serves as a platform for DOJ to directly engage with cities to identify and prioritize resources that will help local communities address their violent crime crises.

Police Executive Research Forum

1120 Connecticut Avenue NW, Suite 930
Washington, DC 20036
(202) 466-7820
email: clitten@policeforum.org
website: www.policeforum.org

The Police Executive Research Forum (PERF) is an independent research organization that focuses on critical issues in policing. Since its founding in 1976, PERF has identified best practices on fundamental issues such as reducing police use of force, developing community policing and problem-oriented policing, using technologies to deliver police services to the community, and evaluating crime reduction strategies. PERF strives to advance professionalism in policing and to improve the delivery of police services through the exercise of strong national leadership, public debate of police and criminal justice issues, and research and policy development.

Vera Institute of Justice
34 35th Street
Suite 4-2A
Brooklyn, NY 11232
(212) 334-1300
email: available via contact form on website
website: www.vera.org

The Vera Institute of Justice works in partnership with local, state, and national government officials to create change from within. It works with other organizations that share its vision to tackle the most pressing injustices of the day—from the causes and consequences of mass incarceration, racial disparities, and the loss of public trust in law enforcement, to the unmet needs of the vulnerable, the marginalized, and those harmed by crime and violence. The result: justice systems that ensure fairness, promote safety, and strengthen communities.

Bibliography

Books

Michelle Alexander. *The New Jim Crow* (Revised). New York, NY: The New Press, 2016.

Radley Balko. *The Rise of the Warrior Cop. The Militarization of America's Police Forces*. New York, NY: PublicAffairs, 2013.

Paul Butler. *Chokehold: Policing Black Men*. New York, NY: The New Press, 2018.

Jordan T. Camp. *Policing the Planet: Why the Policing Crisis Led to Black Lives Matter.* Brooklyn, NY: Verso Books, 2016.

David Correia. *Police: A Field Guide*. Brooklyn, NY: Verso Books, 2018.

Angela J. Davis. *Policing the Black Man: Arrest, Prosecution, and Imprisonment.* New York, NY: Vintage, 2017.

Matthew Horace and Ron Harris. *The Black and the Blue: A Cop Reveals the Crimes, Racism, and Injustice in America's Law Enforcement*. New York, NY: Hachette Book Group, 2018.

Thomas Jackson. *Policing Ferguson, Policing America: What Really Happened—and What the Country Can Learn from It.* New York, NY: Skyhorse Publishing, 2017.

Charles M. Katz and Edward R. Maguire. *Transforming the Police: Thirteen Key Reforms*. Long Grove, IL: Waveland Press, 2020.

Steve Pomper. *De-Policing America: A Street Cop's View of the Anti-Police State*. Nashville, TN: Post Hill Press, 2018.

Andrea Ritchie. *Invisible No More: Police Violence Against Black Women and Women of Color*. Boston, MA: Beacon Press, 2017.

Maya Schenwar, Joe Macare, Alana Yu-lan Price, and Alicia Garza. *Who Do You Serve, Who Do You Protect? Police Violence and Resistance in the United States*. Chicago, IL: Haymarket Books, 2016.

Stuart Schrader. *Badgers Without Borders: How Global Counterinsurgency Transformed American Policing*. Oakland, CA: University of California Press, 2019.

Micol Seigel. *Violence Work: State Power and the Limits of Police*. Durham, NC: Duke University Press, 2018.

Sarah A. Seo. *Policing the Open Road*. Cambridge, MA: Harvard University Press, 2019.

Keeanga-Yamahtta Taylor. *From #BlackLivesMatter to Black Liberation*. Chicago, IL: Haymarket Books, 2016.

Alex S. Vitale. *The End of Policing*. Brooklyn, NY: Verso Books, 2017.

Kristian Williams. *Our Enemies in Blue: Police and Power in America*. Stirling, UK: AK Press, 2015.

Periodicals and Internet Sources

Chauncey Alcorn, "Body Cam Industry Is Under Pressure After Deaths of George Floyd and Breonna Taylor," CNN, September 28, 2020, https://www.cnn.com/2020/09/26/business/breonna-taylor-george-floyd-axon-body-cams/index.html

Luke Barr, "US Police Agencies Having Trouble Hiring, Keeping Officers, According to a New Survey," ABC News, September 17, 2019, https://abcnews.go.com/Politics/us-police-agencies-trouble-hiring-keeping-officers-survey/story?id=65643752

Evan Casey, "All Wauwatosa Police Could Be Wearing Body Cameras by the End of the Year. Here's What to Know," *Milwaukee Journal Sentinel*, October 1, 2020, https://www

.jsonline.com/story/communities/west/news/wauwatosa/2020/10/01/wauwatosa-police-officers-could-wearing-body-cameras-end-2020/5878771002/

Ken Crane, "Viewpoints: The 10,000 Good Things Police Do Each Day That You Don't Often See," AZ Central, August 12, 2016, https://www.azcentral.com/story/opinion/op-ed/2016/08/12/police-officers-positive-work-crane/88410664/

Michelle Crouch, "45 Things Police Officers Want You to Know," *Reader's Digest*, August 9, 2018, https://www.rd.com/list/police-officers/

Tim Fitzsimons and Mike Hixenbaugh, "4 Houston Police Fired After Body Cam Shows Nicolas Chavez Killing," NBC News, September 11, 2020, https://www.nbcnews.com/news/us-news/4-houston-police-fired-after-body-cams-shows-nicolas-chavez-n1239854

Steve Inskeep, "Al Sharpton: Policing in America Will Change Because of George Floyd's Death," NPR, September 28, 2020, https://www.npr.org/2020/09/28/917656974/al-sharpton-policing-in-america-will-change-because-of-george-floyds-death

Tom Jackman, "Judge Rules Federal Law Enforcement Commission Violates Law, Orders Work Stopped as Attorney General Prepares to Issue Report," *Washington Post*, October 1, 2020, https://www.washingtonpost.com/crime-law/2020/10/01/judge-rules-federal-law-enforcement-commission-violates-law-orders-work-stopped-attorney-general-prepares-issue-report/

Sam Levin, "White Supremacists and Militias Have Infiltrated Police Across US, Report Says," *Guardian*, August 27, 2020, https://www.theguardian.com/us-news/2020/aug/27/white-supremacists-militias-infiltrate-us-police-report

German Lopez, "American Policing Is Broken. Here's How to Fix It," Vox, September 1, 2017, https://www.vox.com/policy-and-politics/2016/11/29/12989428/police-shooting-race-crime

Mike Masciadrelli, "Springfield City Leaders Host Virtual Discussion on Improving Police-Community Relations," 22 News WWLP, September 26, 2020, https://www.wwlp.com/news/local-news/hampden-county/springfield-city-leaders-host-virtual-discussion-on-improving-police-community-relations/

Geoff Mulvihill, "Police Departments Seeing Modest Cuts, but not 'Defunding,'" *Spokesman-Review*, October 1, 2020, https://www.spokesman.com/stories/2020/oct/01/police-departments-seeing-modest-cuts-but-not-defu/

William Poor, "Police Body Cameras Don't Tell the Whole Story. This Experiment Shows It," The Verge, August 31, 2020, https://www.theverge.com/21378159/police-brutality-protests-body-cameras-video-surveillance-black-lives-matter

Justin T. Ready and Jacob T. N. Young, "The Unfulfilled Potential of Police Body Cameras in the Era of Black Lives Matter," Slate, October 1, 2020, https://slate.com/technology/2020/10/black-lives-matter-police-body-cameras.html

Mychal Denzel Smith, "Rough Justice: How America Became Over-Policed," *New Republic*, June 5, 2018, https://newrepublic.com/article/148304/rough-justice-america-over-policed

Alice Speri, "Unredacted FBI Document Sheds Light on White Supremacist Infiltration of Law Enforcement," The Intercept, September 29, 2020, https://theintercept.com/2020/09/29/police-white-supremacist-infiltration-fbi/

Frank Stoltze, "'I've Never Seen This Before' — Police-Community Relations Are at a Low Point," LAist, October 1, 2020, https://laist.com/2020/10/01/police_community_relations_los_angeles_low_point.php

Kelsey Thompson, "Pflugerville Police Department Unveils Public Assistance Programs for Vulnerable Populations," *Community Impact Newspaper*, October 1, 2020, https://communityimpact.com/austin/round-rock-pflugerville-hutto/public-safety/2020/10/01/pflugerville-police-department-unveils-public-assistance-programs-for-vulnerable-populations/

Index

E

F

G

H

I

J

K

L

M

U

V

W

Y

Z